Rise
to the Occasion

*From Tragedy to Triumph;
A Christian Perspective*

JEANINE SENEROTE VALENTI

WESTBOW
PRESS®
A DIVISION OF THOMAS NELSON
& ZONDERVAN

This book is a work of non-fiction. Unless otherwise noted, the author and the publisher make no explicit guarantees as to the accuracy of the information contained in this book and in some cases, names of people and places have been altered to protect their privacy.

WestBow Press books may be ordered through booksellers or by contacting:

WestBow Press
A Division of Thomas Nelson & Zondervan
1663 Liberty Drive
Bloomington, IN 47403
www.westbowpress.com
844-714-3454

ISBN: 978-1-6642-9288-8 (sc)
ISBN: 978-1-6642-9289-5 (hc)
ISBN: 978-1-6642-9503-2 (e)

Library of Congress Control Number: 2023904525

Print information available on the last page.

WestBow Press rev. date: 05/02/2023

To Rick, whose skepticism motivated me to write this spiritual memoir.

Calling on all Drivers: An important Public Service Announcement on behalf of the hundreds of thousands of people who drive from wheelchairs all across America:

When parking in a handicap spot, or next to one: Please be mindful that you do not park on the blue diagonal-lined ramp spots that accompany most handicap spots. People who drive from their power wheelchairs need this ramp space in order to safely get back into their cars. Even taking up just an inch of their ramp space can make it impossible to enter their vans.

Wheelchair drivers have all spent too much precious time in parking lots waiting for people to return to their cars. No one parks carelessly on purpose; we are usually in a hurry and don't want to take the extra few seconds to adjust our cars. Many drivers never wondered why the diagonal blue lines exist. Through education, we can all make a difference! Please…SPREAD THE WORD!! Ambulatory but handicapped drivers are the biggest offenders!

> This is why you don't park in the striped area of a handicapped parking zone.
> Please share, thanks.

Contents

Introduction xi

Chapter 1   Blessed Beyond All Measure 1
Chapter 2   The Early Years 8
Chapter 3   Bible Fundamentals 17
Chapter 4   Bible 101, New Testament 30
Chapter 5   Nothing Can Separate Us from the Love of God......36
Chapter 6   November 23, 2001 46
Chapter 7   My Journey toward Healing 55
Chapter 8   To Church or Not to Church 67
Chapter 9   Why Bad Things Happen to Good People 72
Chapter 10   The Miracles of Jesus 87
Chapter 11   My Journey Forward 93
Chapter 12   That Was Then, This Is Now 98
Chapter 13   2016 Highlights 107
Chapter 14   2017 Highlights 111
Chapter 15   2018 Highlights 116
Chapter 16   2020 Highlights.. 118
Chapter 17   A Tribute to Tom 125
Chapter 18   Understanding Heaven 139

Introduction

Who is Jeanine Senerote Valenti? I hope you have many answers to this question by the conclusion of this memoir. There are two parts of my life—the pre-injured part that holds many wonderful memories and the post-injured part that has been transformative and gratifying in ways I could never have imagined or, especially, predicted. My pre-injured life was my "Plan A" when I thought that *I* controlled my destiny. That treasured plan ended abruptly on November 23, 2001, at 2:09 p.m., when I became a quadriplegic in one cruel second.

I have replayed that one brutally unfair second in my head over and over again, imagining a variety of improved outcomes. But the outcome never changes. It always plays back in slow motion. The end result relentlessly disappoints, always hurts, and leaves me in disbelief. I endured one second of trauma, yet it took three years to quell the PTSD I suffered. The fear and regret would jolt me out of a dead sleep, leaving my heart to race. I often think about the real heroes in life—our war veterans, police officers and first responders, who have accumulated years of traumatic experiences and, somehow, are expected to be strong enough to carry the heavy burdens of yesterday while brilliantly executing the duties of today. This seems like cruel and unusual punishment, which brings me to the day after Thanksgiving of 2001.

It was on this dreadful day of November 23rd that "Plan B" was forced into action—just one week before my thirty-seventh birthday. On this day, I became dependent on everyone and everything. I needed family to rally around me, to root for me, and to pray unceasingly. I needed nurses and doctors to care for my every need and machines to pump medicines into my bloodstream, and a respirator to assist me with every breath. So, I stand before you now, having proudly written all I want you to know about my life through this detailed account.

This accomplishment is even more celebratory when I recognize that my dominant right hand can only hold light objects, but it does not open, and I cannot move any fingers on my right hand with the exception of my thumb, which is typical of my injury location. I thank God every day for equipping me with an inexorable drive to get things done. Without this quality, which has never failed me, this account of my life would never have found its way onto these once blank pages.

My motivation for writing a book has remained steady throughout the years because of the responses I get from strangers. I cover a lot of ground in a day and "run into" a lot of people. Given that I'm permanently wheelchair dependent, my husband, Tom, cringes when I say, "Honey, you will never guess who I ran into today!" The deer-in-the-headlights expression on his face imagines me knocking people over like pins that fall victim to a heavy bowling ball when hurled into action.

I guess it's because I always have my power chair on maximum speed and navigate with confidence. Despite wanting to "slow down," I whizz by everyone as if they are standing still. I cannot help myself. I am a mover and a shaker, an enormous undertaker, trying to make the world a better place than it was when I entered it.

From the "many" people I encounter, I get sweet smiles, kind offers of assistance, and curious and innocent stares from young children. My favorite reaction was from a two-year-old toddler, who observed me gliding through the halls of Kessler Institute. When I entered the atrium, our eyes met and he shouted, "*Wwwwhhhheeeee!*"

My second favorite reaction came from a parishioner of my parish, a retired police captain. He said to me, "I see how fast you drive that wheelchair. You might need this for your car." And he handed me a PBA card! We laughed together, but I had to inform him that, although I might operate both of my vehicles fast, I do have a perfect driving record.

As I go through my everyday routines in life, the most frequent reaction I get from people is, "*God bless you.*" And that response is precisely why I am writing *Rise to the Occasion*. Well-meaning, compassionate strangers look me in the eye and say, "God bless you."

I always respond confidently with the same four words, triumphantly declaring, "*Thank you. He has!*"

And sadly, the potential for any meaningful conversation ends before it can even begin. As victims of our fast-paced world, we are usually off running somewhere at least five minutes behind schedule. This book allows me the luxury of more time to explain the second part of my response—that God *has* blessed me. It is the importance and awesomeness of the *how* he has blessed me that I so enthusiastically and wholeheartedly write.

Chapter 1

Blessed Beyond All Measure

By 1955, my parents had three boys, the youngest of whom broke their hearts in 1958, when he died of leukemia at the innocent and defenseless age of three. In 1964, their older sons, or my future brothers, Tommy, fourteen, and Eddie, twelve, learned that they were going to be big brothers once again, and they were happy. But my parents—well, not so much. For them, life was just getting easier, and they did not have the strength or energy to start over. Lucky for us, our parents were devout Catholics who obeyed Cardinal Law, which forbade abortions.

Hold on to your seat and journey with me. Turn your calendars back to where so many of my unborn blessings began—in utero, 1964.

Mom worked for Dr. Ralph Schwartz, an ob-gyn in Brooklyn. This doctor was keeping a secret from my mother. Doctors of today would never legally get away with this unscathed, but we will not reveal that secret until a little later.

Blessing Number One: Fertilization

Have you ever heard the expression "you are one in a million"? This saying is very inaccurate. On average, there are a hundred million sperm that are sent out on a call to make one baby. Only *one* of those hundred million microscopic critters are needed to fertilize one egg. Sometimes that one fertilized egg will split, creating identical twins, or sometimes the woman releases two eggs in one month and both eggs get fertilized by two different sperm, creating fraternal twins. Regardless of whether you are a twin or were born solo, you beat incredible odds by that one sperm finding the egg the fastest. The sperm that fertilized your egg won the sprint if you are a boy or a marathon if you are a girl.

Male sperm swim faster than female sperm, but they don't live as long. The female swimmers are slower but have much more endurance. If you are alive to read this book, you, too, were blessed beyond all measure before you were even born.

Blessing Number Two: Escaping a Dangerous Drug

Mom was well into her pregnancy when she began spotting, which was a commonly known forewarning of spontaneous abortions or miscarriages. Unlike most moms, this possibility did not upset her. Her conscience would be clear should nature take its course. Dr. Schwartz always said that spontaneous abortions were "Mother Nature's way of taking care of 'imperfections.'" Mom did what every good churchgoing, God-fearing Catholic should do—nothing.

Before long, doing nothing was not enough. She then started running up and down every staircase that naturally stood in her path, hoping to encourage Mother Nature a bit.

At that time, a drug called diethylstilbestrol, or DES, was available to Mom. This drug was used in the 1960s to prevent spontaneous abortions. My mother chose *not* to take this drug, and that is where my second blessing begins. Had Mom taken that drug, I would have had a 40 percent chance of developing ovarian cancer between the ages of ten and forty.

Blessing Number Three: Escaping a Second Birth Defect

The third blessing that was bestowed upon me/us was tied into that secret Dr. Schwartz was keeping from Mom. My mother was carrying twins! Dr. Schwartz did not have the heart to tell Jeanne about the twins, because the thought of having just one child kept her up at night (and running up and down staircases).

My third blessing occurred while in utero and at birth. Jeanne made it to full term unaware she was having twins. This still perplexes me to this day. We were Mom's fourth pregnancy, not her first. She always emphasized how big she was during this pregnancy and occasionally reflected on how abnormally swollen she was during her last trimester. She always emphatically maintained the shock of learning she had given birth to twins. The story I always heard—and it never changed—was that my sister was born first. Mom thought she was done, but Dr. Schwartz said, "Hold on, Jeannie. We still have another one!"

"Another one?!" She then let out a very opinionated, out-of-character utterance. And with that, Mom passed out, her blood pressure dropped dangerously low, and she fell hard into a coma.

Lucky for all involved, she woke up twenty-four hours later. I was never able to get an accurate account of what must have been a nail-biting, prayer-filled twenty-four hours.

Mom gave everyone quite a scare. At that time, fathers were not permitted to stay with their wives during delivery—I assure you that was a *man*-made rule. Dad went home to be with my brothers for the wait.

When Dr. Schwartz called my dad, he said, "Congratulations, Mr. Senerote! You are now the father of twin girls!"

My father responded, "There must be some mistake. Go back and count again!"

My fraternal twin sister turned out to be very developmentally delayed (hence the spotting). For some unknown—and certainly undeserving—reason, I was born well-developed and at least of

3

average intelligence. To be clear, *before I was born, I was blessed beyond all measure.*

Our family did not realize how handicapped or mentally incapacitated Francine was until she began kindergarten in 1969. My mother suspected that something was wrong. But our pediatrician did not give my mom enough credit for really knowing her children. Instead of further exploring Mom's claims by testing my sister, the pediatrician told her that, in comparison to me, Fran was slow, but when compared with most other children, she was right on target. That sounded great at the time, but the analysis carried no weight because Francine was never compared to other children her age.

When we entered kindergarten, it was decided we should be split up between the two kindergarten classes. Francine had never had to be anywhere without me. Our separation was an experiment; she would either flourish on her own or fail. When Fran started failing, she was given permission to join my class to see if this would make a difference.

To everyone's disappointment, Francine remained behind in kindergarten. She was never able to mainstream into an age-appropriate academic level again.

Her life has been good, but she ultimately ended up in a group home at the young age of twenty-two. I link my sister's entry in the group home with tragedy because our mother died on March 31, 1987, from lung cancer at the heartbreaking age of just fifty-nine. By the time I graduated from Rutgers with a BA in Spanish and education, she was already gone—something I never saw coming.

From Mom's first symptom to her last breath, only two months to the day had gone by—February 1, to March 31, 1987. Her lung cancer was not detected until it had spread to her liver.

I learned a lot from my mother in a short twenty-two years, and I was lucky to have her in my life. I laugh at all the times I have used the quirky quotes she gave me along the way and chuckle under my breath at the many times I have sounded just like her. Talking about Mom through the years has kept her alive and influential to my family, especially my children. My daughter, Marisa, inherited

Mom's talent for playing the piano. My youngest son, Tommy, inherited his grandmother's talent for sewing and crocheting and his grandfather's talent for drawing and painting.

My Uncle Robert had an even greater talent for drawing, but never treated himself to art lessons of any kind. Dad and Robert's generation (known as the Greatest Generation through a book published by Tom Brokaw of NBC News) were too busy fighting wars and trying to survive, rather than indulging in anything as frivolous or superfluous as art lessons.

My mom volunteered for the ARC of Middlesex. Its name has since changed to be more politically correct, but then ARC stood for the Association for Retarded Citizens. Today, it is just the ARC of Middlesex. Back in the '70s and '80s, the waiting list for residential services, or group homes, was hopelessly long. We were consistently told that Francine's situation was not dire enough and that she would not find placement until both parents became deceased.

After we'd given up hope that my parents would be relieved of their heavy burdens within their lifetimes, a state senator started working at Mom's company. My mom saw the state senator as a great opportunity or "connection" to get Francine a higher placement on the group home waiting list. She wrote a letter to Jack. This letter enabled Francine to be interviewed for a placement in a group home in Jamesburg on School House Road. This hope was very real, as it was promising and exciting. I wanted to see Mom get her life back, claim it as hers, and start having fun again. We all loved Francine and never neglected her. Our intention for placing her in a group home was to allow her to grow up with friends her age in similar situations.

Her very bad behavior was constant around our mother, and it was wearing her down. She was always exhausted and had no time for herself. Between her full-time job, cooking, grocery shopping, washing laundry, and constantly trying to help Franny learn her lessons and life skills, there was nothing left for Mom's needs.

The acceptance letter came in the mail. But before we had time to absorb its implications for a better life and celebrate, Mom found out that same week that she may have cancer. Two months later, she was gone, and Francine was still living at home with an "indefinite" postponement of a move-in date for her new group home. The day after Mom died, April 1, 1987, I got a call from the ARC informing me of Francine's move-in date scheduled in just two weeks! I couldn't help but believe that Mom was "up there" working for the well-being of her family.

With wisdom and retrospect, I have grown to realize how hard Mom was on me growing up. She gave me lots of chores to do and was never happy with how I performed them. Her expectations were high, and I never seemed to accomplish enough to satisfy her. When I was just five years old, she would praise me as "Mommy's little helper," and she would give me a nut picker and have me scrape out the dirt that made the grout look dirty on the kitchen floor. By the time I was ten, she would leave out ingredients for dinner that night. I always had to do the dishes and wash the hundred jalousie slat windows in our family room. That was very labor intensive, but I always ached to make my mother happy.

By my sophomore year of high school, I was doing my own ironing and laundry. My very first job happened when I was just thirteen years old working for a doctor's wife, cleaning her house and the adjoining doctor's office. As an experienced Mom, I think this job was an extraordinary task for a thirteen-year-old. Mom never revealed whether this made her proud. But as an adult now, looking back, I am impressed with myself. Cleaning for my meticulous mom for all those years enabled me to clean a medical office and a doctor's home well enough to please the high cleaning requirements of a medical doctor.

At sixteen, I was the hostess for Rustler Steakhouse. And by that summer, for an entire year, I worked as a typist for Royal Foods in Woodbridge, New Jersey where my mother worked. By then, with only 1 typing course under my belt, I was typing at eighty-five words per minute. My typing skills always made getting secretarial jobs easy, and I worked every summer as a "Kelly girl temp" until I had children. When I began to teach high school, I worked every summer as someone's secretary. I earned top dollar with what is now Kelly Services because I always got raving reviews from the companies I served in corporate America.

I have grown to give my mom a lot of credit for my enormous emotional strength today. She never went out of her way to make things easy for me. She was not affectionate, that was not her style. I always craved affection and praise and worked to try and earn them.

When I became a mom, I made it *my* style of parenting. I never wanted my kids to feel like they weren't good "enough" to be loved. I know that a mother's love is unconditional, but I wanted them to *feel* loved. I wanted them to *feel* admired and valued. I wanted to be more than their "mother." Anyone can be a *mother*, so to me, *mom* is much more endearing and heartwarming to the ear. Every time my own children call me Mom, a warm ray of sunshine shoots through my heart like the fast-acting fuse of a firework right before it bursts into flame and explodes into vibrant colors.

Chapter 2

The Early Years

My spiritual journey began very young, as I was brought up in the church. Every Sunday and Holy Day of Obligation, it was a mandatory requirement. My mom was a Southern Baptist, and my dad, a Roman Catholic. Eugene Julius Senerote and Jeanne Rankin were married on April 24,1948. At that time, the Catholic Church denied couples a church wedding who were not both Catholic. Mom and Dad got married in the rectory with a best man, a maid of honor, and parents of the bride and groom.

The newlyweds had a very modest honeymoon in Williamsburg, Virginia, and rented a one-bedroom apartment in Brooklyn New York on New York Ave. stayed in that tiny apartment for the next seven years and began to raise a family. Their three boys, Tommy, Eddie, and Lenny were born within six years of each other, all sharing the one bedroom in the apartment, and Mom and Dad took the pullout couch in the living room. It always impressed me to know that the desk where they paid their bills converted into a kitchen table where they ate their meals.

My parents lived in a modestly furnished apartment. The only decor they had was a picture or two, which were hung much too high on the walls. Dad was a mail carrier, who worked in the Empire State Building in New York City and my mother worked nights as a typist for an author in Brooklyn. Their salaries added up to a very modest living, yet she never led me to believe that they wanted for anything.

Mom was born into the projects in Nashville, Tennessee, on May 2, 1927. She graduated from Birmingham High School in Alabama in June 1945. That summer, she moved to Brooklyn, New York, where she landed a job as the secretary to Branch Rickey, manager of the Brooklyn Dodgers.

This was a very historic time in Dodgers baseball history. At twenty-eight years old, Jackie Robinson was the first black athlete to play in Major League Baseball. On April 15, 1947, as Jackie stepped on to Ebbits Field to represent the Brooklyn Dodgers, he broke the color barrier that had been in place for over ninety years since baseball's start in the 1840's. Mom mentioned how much she admired Jackie—not only for his talent but also for the humility and grace with which he handled great animosity and tremendous cruelty, simply for being a black man with extraordinary talent, following his dreams.

When the movie *42* came out with Chadwick Boseman as Jackie Robinson and Harrison Ford as Branch Rickey, I saw these Hollywood Actors trying to portray what Mom had meant. Jackie was a real "class act." He suffered terrible abuse and displayed unprecedented courage by not giving in to fear as he endured thousands of death threats by mail and inhumane treatment on the field at the hands of Dodger fans and even among his own team players. It was a different time, for sure. What a thrill it was for me, as I hung on every word of the dialogue in *42*. I would count how many times Branch Rickey called out for his secretary "JeAnne," on his intercom and listen to "my mother's" response! Her character made a split-second appearance as she and others stood around Mr. Robinson on that historic day in April when he signed his baseball contract! This day was only nine days before Mom was to wed. This was, indeed, a very exciting point in her life.

When the Brooklyn Dodgers made their move to California to become the Los Angeles Dodgers, Branch invited my mom to go with the team, but my dad did not want to go. He did not want to forfeit his seniority. He was a mail carrier assigned to eleven floors of the Empire State Building, never having to wonder or care what the weather was like during the hottest days of summer or the harshest months of winter.

By the time Lenny, the youngest of my three older brothers, was just two and a half years old, he was diagnosed with leukemia. In the 1950s, leukemia was a certain death sentence. My parents were devastated and leaned on their faith and trust in God to get them through this heartbreaking situation. Lenny died eleven months later at three and a half years old. But his dying words were a gift from God to reassure my parents that Lenny was in good hands and never alone as he journeyed to heaven.

As my youngest brother was slipping in and out of consciousness in his hospital bed, Lenny had a lucid moment and asked Mom, "Can I go for a walk?"

Mom said, "No, sweetheart. I'm afraid you can't. You are very sick."

But Lenny looked up and pointed to a corner of the ceiling and said, "But the man in the corner with the green coat wants me to take a walk with him and … I want to go." Lenny then closed his eyes and breathed his last breath. Mom always felt that the man was Jesus himself meeting and accompanying Lenny into His Father's kingdom.

In Matthew 19:14 (NIV), Jesus said, "Let the little children come to me, and do not hinder them, for the Kingdom of Heaven belongs to such as these."

Francine and I did not come into this life until six years later. As I stated, by the time my brother Tommy was sixteen years old and Eddie was thirteen, we lived in Brooklyn on Raleigh Place around the corner from our Holy Cross Church on Church Avenue. Raleigh Place was within walking distance of the church.

Even though we moved to New Jersey by the time I was seven, I still remember that church. I remember the wax on the wooden seats, which were all bench style. I remember the dimmed lighting that hung from the ceiling. The light fixtures hung down in a tubelike cylinder. Each vertical light fixture had a black vertical cross in front and back; but the end of the cross did not end abruptly. It curved back down around itself to form a fish shape, an early symbol of Christianity. I still remember the red carpet runners that ran in between each section of seats and up on the altar. I am amazed I can still smell the church and still remember the feeling the Mass gave me. The altar always had different flowers arranged in vases. I remember the songs we sang, the veils the women wore over their heads, and the dressy clothes worn by the parishioners. Whenever the priest announced the transformation of the Eucharist into the body of Christ, an altar boy would ring a bell symbolizing the holy transformation of unconsecrated bread to a holy symbol of Christ.

Mom had a great talent for sewing. She made all of our clothing and would dress us alike. This added to our "cuteness," and parishioners would always smile warmly and compliment my outfit and appearance. I hope to go back soon one day to visit and attend a Mass.

My parents were both hard workers. And by the time Lenny was born, they were able to buy a duplex brownstone on Raleigh Place in Brooklyn, New York, which was in the Flatbush section. I did not know this until later, but my grandfather Guy Rankin died while I was in utero. My maternal grandparents lived in the Catskills, in a tiny village of Walton, New York.

My grandmother, Frances Rankin, now a widow, came to live with my mom to help with the twins. Grandma was another rich blessing in my life. I lived with my grandmother until she died when I was ten. I loved her dearly. She had a bad heart condition so she could never do anything dramatic or physical with me. She lived on the top floor of our duplex in Brooklyn. We lived in the house downstairs. I would visit her daily, and she would spend hours reading to me.

I can still recall sitting on her lap as she watched the *Galloping Gourmet* and *Kids Say the Darndest Things* with Art Linkletter. The highlight of *The Galloping Gourmet* was watching the expression on the gourmet cook's face when he ate his own meal. His eyes would roll to the back of his head in ecstasy, and I always wished I could be at his table eating what he was eating.

Every Sunday, she would watch the Reverend Bob Schuller. She would share her coffee with me, and I would sit on her lap knowing I was loved beyond all worldly measure. I can only hope and pray, starting today, that I will make my future grandchildren feel a love as strong emanating from me, with the same intensity I felt from my grandmother's strong, deep love for me.

I have very warm memories of my childhood in Brooklyn. There were many kids of all ages who lived on our block, some of whom I am still friends with today. I had my set of friends who had older siblings who belonged to another group of friends that would gather together as a different group. It seemed like all the groups would play outside all day in the summer. I remember playing hide-and-seek, playing with my dolls, playing with blocks, and riding tricycles on the sidewalk where it was safe. I remember drawing hopscotch grids on the sidewalk with chalk and the daily Mister Softee truck, which arrived in the late afternoon / early evening. I recall the driver's face like it was yesterday. I would order my favorite ice cream almost every time—a vanilla cartwheel, which was a round scalloped ice cream sandwich. As he handed me the cartwheel, he would say, "Thank you!" And I would always smile and say, "No. Thank *you!*"

We got called in for meals. And after that, some groups would be right back at it. Since I was so young, more often than not, I couldn't go back out. I got a bath, dessert, and went to bed by 7:00 or 7:30—when it was still light out! Since my room didn't have a window in it, the daylight did not distract me. I often fell asleep to a record player narrating the story of "Hansel and Gretel" or "Snow White." My grandmother would sometimes rub my back in a figure eight motion till I fell asleep. Only God knows how much I loved my grandmother. Only God knows if I will be equally as blessed to come to know and love my grandchildren like my grandmother came to know and love me. It's a role I have always looked forward to and understood as holding great potential.

Brooklyn holds so many endearing and enduring memories for me. There was a neighbor who lived very close to Church Avenue near the corner laundromat. He must have worked for a toy company.

Every year, he would fill his trunk up with doll babies of every size and variation and would let the little girls on the block pick out any doll they wanted, free of charge. That neighbor has since passed, but I am sure he never lived to realize how special his generosity was and how it affected the smallest residents of Raleigh Place.

There was Motorcycle Pete, who was young—around twenty-eight or thirty years old I would guess. He loved throwing kids up in the air and catching them. He had a newborn baby daughter named Jennifer. I remember the pillow he had for her. It was white with a clear shiny white ruffle all around it, and in pink thread, "Jennifer" had been sown on in cursive. To this day, I love the name because it reminds me of that beautiful pillow and the young, handsome, strong dad who would throw us up in the air and take the older kids for rides on his motorcycle.

An older group of kids, all boys, played football and stickball in the streets. They were rough, tough, and didn't seem to like little girls around. They would curse loudly all day long. I was young and innocent, but I knew every curse word (though I had no idea what each meant).

The moms were friends as well. We walked to church, and we walked to school. By the time I was in first grade, my mom allowed me to walk home alone from the mini school affiliated with PS 181.

I remember in first and second grade being allowed to walk home for lunch and come back. It was a beautiful time of my life. My brothers were still living at home, but they lived upstairs with my grandmother. I know music from the '60s because my brothers were always playing cool rock and roll music. When I was very young, Tommy and Eddie would bring their girlfriends home and entertain them in the basement, and I was always interfering with their dates. I often would run down the stairs, wanting to be with them, not understanding why they would not want or enjoy my company. After all, everyone seemed to be my friend when I was four. Adults always wanted to hug and kiss me. Why didn't my teenage brothers?

My brother Eddie used to say, "Hey, Jeanine, do me a favor. Walk to the corner and tell me if it's snowing." Or he'd say, "Jeanine, do me a favor. Go play in traffic"

My oldest brother, Tommy, used to tell me how he loved taking my sister and me for walks in the stroller. He used us as "chick magnets" to pick up girls in the park. Girls would flock to the stroller and marvel at our cuteness. They would always ask my brother if the girls were his, and this would present the perfect opportunity to let these girls know that we were his sisters and that he was single! My brother never thanked me for cooperating so nicely and conforming with the role he cast me in. But for the record, "You are welcome, Tommy!"

Another memory, a sign of the times—my grandmother and mother would make my brothers' beds every morning after they left for work. I had to make my own bed because I was a girl.

During the summer months over the weekends, we would go to nearby beaches. That was my favorite activity. I loved the water and would jump with the waves for hours. Every night, we ate together as a family. My mother was a great cook. And every Sunday my brothers would bring their girlfriends for dinner. I remember Flatbush Avenue and the many shops that were there. My brothers would take me to Coney Island or out to lunch for pizza. Life was so good in the eyes of a four-year-old.

My brother Eddie had a girlfriend named Candy; only unlike her name, she was not sweet. She did not like my mother, and my mother was not fond of her, either. What made me realize that fun fact was the night I took my bowl of chocolate ice cream down to the basement and sat right down between Eddie and Candy on the couch and proceeded to eat my ice cream. Candy noticed my mother's dress that was poised for ironing on Mom's ironing board. Instead of asking me for an outside weather report or suggesting I play in traffic, Candy asked me to dump my ice cream on mom's cleaned but unironed dress. Of course, I refused. Yes of course I told Mom.

That Christmas, Candy bought my mother a gift that she *knew* my mom would *hate*! It was a one-piece purple transparent lingerie with very sheer and wide legs. Each pant leg had a wide purple ruffle at the bottom. Mom thanked Candy—and set out to work on her state-of-the-art sewing machine.

By Candy's next home visit, we were instructed to get ready for bed and to put on our "new" pajamas. Francine and I greeted Candy in our beautiful homemade pajamas that Mom had made for us— purple sleeveless nightgowns with a purple ruffle around the bottom. Each gown was made from the pants of Mom's hideous nightgown! I don't remember Candy's reaction, but I was pretty sure that my new pj's were the payback for Candy suggesting I put ice cream on Mom's green and blue, vertically-striped dress.

Francine and I benefited from Mom's many talents. Besides being a great cook and working hard to maintain an immaculate house, Mom made all our clothes. She made two of everything, all adorable matching outfits that emphasized our cuteness and status as twins. From the leftover scraps of material, she made a quilt—one I still proudly display today on our family room couch. If you were to look through my childhood photo album, you would literally be able to match my outfits with the squares cut from the scraps of fabric leftovers sewn into that quilt. No scraps of clothing or time and talent were ever wasted.

By 1971, racial tension started getting bad in my neighborhood. After the second robbery of the corner candy store and the second storefront window of the record store was shattered, the owners bought a German shepherd to guard the store. It was still getting robbed. I also remember the neighborhood moms sending their nine and ten-year-olds to that same store to purchase cigarettes for them. How times have changed!

I remember that small groups of men would look at me from the street corners with disdain. It was a very different feeling than what I had known. I was used to wonderful expressions on people's faces when they would see me—always smiling, calling me "sweetie" and "honey" and "sugar." But this group looked me up and down wearing expressions that were blatantly ugly, and they would call me "honky." At five years old, I did not know what a honky was, but it was obvious to me that it's meaning wasn't good.

One of the houses at the end of our street was boarded up, and I used to see men come and go out of that house. My mother would tell me to stay away. "Don't go near that house," she would say.

Houses started going up for sale on my block. By the time I was seven years old in February 1972, we had moved to Iselin, New Jersey—forty-one minutes away and where I would spend the next twenty years of my life.

Chapter 3

Bible Fundamentals

In order to understand my spiritual journey, there are things I have to explain about the Bible and its contents. If you identify as a Christian, it remains my hope that what you will learn from this short book may enhance your spirituality. If you identify with a different religion and that religion satisfies you, that is fantastic! My hope for you as an educator is that you gain a better understanding of Christianity. What these next few chapters explain, I hope, will enable you to learn things you never knew or, perhaps, expel any falsehoods or inaccuracies you may have picked up during your life's journey about what it means to be a Christian.

Both the Christian and Jewish religions begin with the Old Testament. The first chapters of the first book of Genesis, chapters 1 through 3, begin with God creating the world.

It's important to know that the God of all humanity had a glorious plan set out for us as his creation. For us, he wanted a life filled with splendid beauty—a world with no sickness, no worries, no crime, no evil of any kind, just a man and a woman, whose descendants and future descendants would populate this beautiful, blissful world. God intended for this world to be perfect in every aspect in ways our humanness can't even fathom. He loved his creation and marveled at it. The different fruits and vegetables that grew in the garden he created were perfect. God made Adam master of all life on the earth (Genesis 1:26, NIV). Their food sources were plentiful, and their requirements were one—to obey God. This should have been *easy* for humankind to follow because God only gave them *one* rule—*not* to eat the fruit from the tree of knowledge of good and evil.

The third chapter of Genesis informs us that Satan came to Adam and Eve in the form of a serpent *from that forbidden tree* and gave Eve the thought that greatly tempted her—if she were to eat the forbidden fruit, she would become "more like God." Eve examined the fruit, saw that it looked good to eat, and tasted it. Adam (the man) decided to follow her and tasted it.

The story continues, but they immediately realized they were naked and felt ashamed. Eve sewed together fig leaves to cover themselves. When God saw this, he knew that Adam and Eve had disobeyed him by eating from that tree. This is the first sin, known as "original sin." Both religions, Christian and Judaism, acknowledge this act of disobedience as the first sin. The next four books, along with Genesis, make up the Torah, which is the most sacred scriptures of the Jewish religion. The Torah focuses on the role of Moses and the laws of God to which Orthodox Jews strictly adhere.

In Genesis, God gets very angry with Adam and Eve and locks them out of the beautiful garden he created for them. They no longer can eat from the tree of life, which made them immortal. The consequences of this "original sin" are quite harsh and still exist today—*thousands* of years later. As a punishment to Eve and all women, the Lord announced "painful childbirth" with "intense suffering" unfolding because of disobedience. Consequently, to punish men, weeds would plague the soil and nonstop weeding would be required so the crops would not choke in their fields. God also revealed that a curse would be placed on the soil, which would grow weeds resulting in thorns and thistles that would consume all human energy to maintain.

In order for Adam and Eve not to have access to the tree of life, they are banished from paradise known as Eden, and their time in this nirvana would come to an end, along with their lives at some point in the future. Humankind would no longer be immortal because humanity would no longer have access to the tree of life.

The first sin known to man (disobedience) is also known to

Catholics as "original sin." The religious belief is that we are all born with original sin, and this sin is removed by baptism and the parental commitment to raise the baby under the knowledge and understanding of God, creator of the world, who loved us so much he sent his only son, Jesus Christ, to dwell among us and, eventually, be crucified as the perfect paschal sacrifice. This is also the mutual goal of the godparents. We will dive into this later.

Catholicism and Judaism all start with Genesis as the recipe of a world created by God. The next four books, Exodus, Leviticus, Numbers, and Deuteronomy accompany Genesis and are considered the most holy and sacred chapters of the Old Testament, known as the Pentateuch or the Torah.

As I read the Bible, my faith increased exponentially. And I want the same for you. Here are some amazing facts I've learned through my Bible studies over the years.

The Christian Bible is divided into two parts—the Old Testament and the New Testament. The Old Testament begins with how the world and mankind were created and the foretelling of a future Messiah who would deliver the Jewish people from a corrupt government and for Christians, through his crucifixion, would atone for all future sin.

The Old Testament of the Bible has different authors. One of the authors is the prophet Isaiah, who often talks about a "future Messiah"—someone who is coming that will free us from sin and death." There were many predictions made hundreds of years before Jesus's birth. One of the greatest prophecies was from Isaiah, who foretold facts about Jesus seven hundred years before his actual birth! Isaiah is the author of thirty-nine of the sixty-six chapters in the book of Isaiah.

Isaiah 7:14 (NIV) reads, "Now a virgin shall conceive a Son and she shall name him Emmanuel" (which means, God is with us). Jesus was so named because the archangel Gabriel instructed Mary to do so when God sent him to her:

But the angel said to her, "Do not be afraid, Mary, you have found favor with God. You will conceive and give birth to a son;

19

you are to call him Jesus. He will be great and will be called the Son of the Most High. The Lord God will give him the throne of his father David, and he will reign over Jacob's descendants forever; his kingdom will never end."

"How can this be, Mary asked the angel, since I am a virgin?"

The angel answered, "The Holy Spirit will come on you, and the power of the Most High will overshadow you. So, the Holy One to be born will be called the Son of God." (Luke 1:30–35, NIV)

And in a passage referred to as "the good news"—John 3:16 (NIV), we read, "For God so loved the world that he gave his one and only son, that whoever believes in Him should not perish, but have eternal life."

Gabriel told her that she was chosen by God to give birth to a boy who would become the Savior of the World, conceived by the "Holy Spirit." He told her that she was to name him Jesus, which means "deliverer, savior." Throughout the New Testament, Jesus is called many names such as Elijah, Emmanuel, Son of God, Savior of the World, the Great "I AM", Yahweh, Jehovah, the Christ, and many more.

Isaiah, among others, made many predictions about a "future Messiah," to be born of a virgin, who would save the lives of millions/billions by taking away their sins. He would be brutally tortured and crucified and would be raised from the dead. The last prophecy was fulfilled by Jesus on the cross when he refused bitter wine offered to him by the guards guarding the cross. After his refusal to drink, he exclaimed, "It is done" (this was the fulfillment of the last prophecy), and he expired.

This was a huge faith builder for me. Seven hundred years before the birth of Jesus, Isaiah, a prophet of God would predict the entire fate of Jesus:

But, oh, how few believe it! Who will listen? To whom will God reveal his saving power? In God's eyes he [Jesus] was like a tender green shoot, sprouting from a root in dry and sterile ground. But in our eyes, there was no attractiveness at all, nothing to make us want him. We despised him and rejected him—a Man of Sorrows, acquainted with bitterest grief. We turned our backs on him and looked the other way when he went by. He was despised, and we did not care.

Yet it was our grief he bore, our sorrows that weighed him down. And we thought his troubles were a punishment from God, for his own! But he was wounded and bruised for our sins. He was beaten that we might have peace; he was lashed—and we were healed! We—every one of us—have strayed away like sheep! We, who left God's path to follow our own. Yet God laid on him the guilt and sins of every one of us!

He was oppressed and we were afflicted yet he never said a word—he was brought as a lamb to the slaughter; and as a sheep before her shearers is dumb, so he stood silent before the ones condemning him. From prison and trial, they led him away to his death. But who among the people that day realized it was their sins that he was dying for that he was suffering their punishment? He was buried like a criminal, but in a rich man's grave but he had done no wrong and had never spoken an evil word. Yet it was the Lord's good plan to bruise him and fill him with grief. However, when his soul had been made an offering for sin, then he shall have a multitude of children and heirs. He shall live again and God's program shall prosper in his hands. And when he sees all that is accomplished by the anguish of his soul, he shall be satisfied. And because of what he has experienced, my righteous servant shall make many to be counted righteous before God, for he shall bear the sins of many. Therefore, I will give him the honors of one who is mighty and great because he has poured out his soul unto death, he was counted as a sinner, and he bore the sins of many, and he pleaded with God for sinners. (Isaiah 53:1–12, NIV)

The faith enhancer for me was that, for Isaiah to make prophecies that would ultimately be fulfilled, Isaiah had to be connected to God.

When I became familiar with Isaiah's prophecies through a Bible study in my forties and how Jesus fulfilled almost every prophecy, I was spiritually happy, complete, fulfilled, and legitimized. This *proved* to me that the Bible is *real*, and the promises of God are trustworthy and true. This proved to me beyond a shadow of a doubt that the Bible had to be divinely inspired by God for our benefit. And how joy-filled I am to know how much God loved us—millions and millions of us who were not even born yet. He loved us enough to give up his only son and allow him to be tortured for our benefit. There *is no greater*, no stronger love that I can even dream of.

We read in John 19:28–30 (NIV), "Jesus knew that everything was now finished because He had fulfilled every prophecy he was born to carry out, he said, 'I'm thirsty.' 2A jar of sour wine was sitting there, so a sponge was soaked in it and put on a hyssop branch and held up to his lips. When Jesus had tasted it and, he said, 'It is finished', and bowed his head and dismissed his spirit."

And in Matthew 26:29 (NIV), Jesus tells his disciples at the last supper, "I will not drink this fruit of the vine from now on until the day I drink it anew with you in my Father's kingdom."

Parallel Ties between Easter and Passover

Because mankind was now exposed to sin and susceptible to it, he needed a way to cleanse these sins away, because they were causing a separation from God.

Leviticus is the third book of the Torah and the third book of the Old Testament. It outlines for the Jewish people the specific remedies necessary for the forgiveness of certain sins. The book of Leviticus was written by a Jewish man named Moses through communication with God in order to outline the acceptable diets of the people—clean eating versus unclean eating. It listed animals which are clean (acceptable) to eat, and those unclean animals that should never be eaten.

Leviticus 11:1–12, for example, outlines instructions on which animals are clean to eat and which animals are unclean. As a summary of a very complicated segment of the Torah, which outlines forbidden as well as unforbidden foods to eat or reject, is when God called on both Moses and Aaron to tell the people of Israel that the animals that may be used for food include any animal with cloven hooves that chews its cud. This means that the following may not be eaten—the camel because it chews the cud but does not have cloven hooves;

the rock badger because, although it chews the cud, it does not have cloven hooves; the hare because, although it chews the cud, it does not have cloven hooves; and the swine because, although it has cloven hooves, it does not chew the cud. You may not eat the meat or even touch the dead bodies of these animals; the people of Israel are told; they are forbidden foods for you.

The beginning chapters of Leviticus explain the regulations of what type of sacrifice is a remedy for which type of sin. The cleansing process almost always includes the blood of an animal. It is important to note that the rules and regulations are extremely complicated and severe. For example, only certain animals were acceptable to be sacrificed for certain sins. Were the offenses intentional or unintentional? If a priest unintentionally sinned, all of his people would be held guilty as well. Only certain animals could be accepted as adequate sacrifice for serious sins. Different animals for different causes had to be killed in different ways, involving the washing of different body parts, specific ways of cutting up the offering, and placement of blood in different areas of the altar. Rams were used, along with bulls, goats, sheep, cows and pigs; turtle doves and pigeons; and, camels. Grain offerings were also made. Only high priests could enter the part of the tabernacle where the blood of the animal could be spread on the altar for atonement of sins. Some animals had to be burnt continuously without the fire ever going out for an established number of days written in Leviticus as law.

All of this was laid out and explained in Leviticus by Moses as instructed from God. Why is this so *important*? For the Jewish people, forgiveness was very hard to obtain, even if the offense was unintentional. God made it known that the Jews were God's chosen people. His favorites among all mankind! Despite this, forgiveness was still difficult to achieve…especially for His Chosen. Sin separated God's people from their Creator.

The Good News: In God's time, when he thought the timing right, he sent a savior, a Messiah, who would take away the sins of the people so they did not have to overcome such complicated situations under such extreme circumstances to be forgiven.

The second book of the Torah is Exodus, which in chapter 12 outlines instructions for God's chosen to obey during Passover: "Then the Lord said to Moses and Aaron: 'From now on this month will be the first and most important of the entire year'" (Exodus 12: 2, NIV). This feast is still celebrated as the most important Jewish feast.

Annually, on the tenth day of this month, each family shall get a lamb. Or if a family is small, let it share the lamb with another small family in the neighborhood. Whether to share in this way depends on the size of the families. This animal shall be a year-old male, either a sheep or goat, without any defects on the evening of the fourteenth day of the month, all these lambs shall be killed and their blood shall be placed on the two side frames of the door of every home and on the panel above the door. Use the blood of the lamb eaten in that home. Everyone shall eat roast lamb at night, with unleavened bread and bitter herbs. The meat must not be eaten raw or boiled but roasted, including the head, legs, heart, and liver. Don't eat any of it the next day; if all is not eaten that night, burn what is left.

Exodus 12:14–15 explains that the Israelites are to celebrate Passover each year throughout generations forever. This is a permanent law to remind the people of Israel of this fatal night. The celebration shall last seven days. For that entire period, the people are to eat only bread made without yeast; anyone who disobeys this rule at any time during the seven days of the celebration shall be excommunicated from Israel. We read in Exodus 12:46 (NIV), "You shall, all of you who eat each lamb eat it together in one house and not carry it outside and *do not break any of its bones.*"

I am explaining these laws because understanding them leads to the parallels between what was Passover to the Jews and Easter celebration for Christians.

Our Christian Easter is directly related to the Jewish Passover celebration still carried out by the Jews of today. Our two celebrations are intertwined; and understanding how they are related is another faith builder for me. It causes me to feel deeply loved by God because through his son, God makes it so much easier to qualify for eternal paradise. I hope these next few pages can have the same effect for you!

Three days before Passover Jews would go out and choose their perfect, unblemished male lamb to be sacrificed as God outlined in Exodus 12. It had to be an unblemished, one-year-old male. That very day when Jews were choosing their sacrificial lambs, Jesus, at the age of thirty-three, rode into Jerusalem on a donkey, making himself available to the people for slaughter. God had communicated with him that the time of his sacrifice had come. Jesus is considered to be the perfect paschal (Easter) sacrifice. Jesus understood what he was doing and prayed that God's will be fulfilled, but if it the cup could be taken from him, let it be taken from him. Ultimately, though, let God's will be done.

During his "last supper" with his disciples, Jesus made various predictions, which all came to pass. He knew who would betray him, leading to his arrest. He knew who would deny knowing him out of fear of persecution. And he broke bread with his disciples, saying that the broken bread represented his body, and the red wine represented his blood, both of which would be given up for you and me. Jesus wanted us to break bread and drink wine as spiritual gifts that Jesus Christ is providing for us as a way of cleansing our sins.

In the New Testament, specifically John 6:52–57 (NIV) Jesus says to his disciples, "Truly, truly I say to you unless you eat the flesh and drink the blood of the son of man, you have no life in you." And in John: 6:54 (ESV), he says, "Whoever eats my flesh and drinks my blood has eternal life, and I will raise him up on the last day."

Before he hung that cross, he suffered unimaginable pain. He was stripped of his clothing, whipped repeatedly and mocked relentlessly by the crowd. With agonizing open flesh wounds from his flogging, he was forced to carry his own cross to the place where the townspeople would gather to watch Jesus's suffering play out to the end. They would hurl sarcastic and undignified remarks at him as the guards nailed his hands and feet to the wood and erected the cross on a spot where many people were beheaded or crucified before him. This is mentioned in all 4 Gospels of the New Testament. The place was called Golgotha, in Aramaic, which means "place of the skull". Located on the outskirts of Jerusalem, Christians refer to this place as

Calvary. Today, a church was built over this holy site. It is the Church of the Holy Sepulchre, where 4 million people visit this site yearly.

As Jesus hung on that cross, he became every sin known to man. Once crucified, he descended into hell for three days. On that third day, he rose again in fulfillment of ancient scriptures and prophecy. If we believe that Jesus is the Son of God, he became every sin known to man so, through our belief in him, we could carry our future sin and wipe it out through his death. He literally died so our sins could die with him because he linked our sins with his sacrificed blood.

I am not asking you to take my word for it. My word means nothing. But God's word means everything, and this interested me greatly when I was studying the Bible. Jesus holds many titles. One is the Perfect Paschal Sacrifice. This fascinated me because it proved to me more completely that Jesus's role did not just "happen"; nor was it because of a "delusional somebody" who thought he was God.

In Exodus, God instructed the Jewish people to go to the market and select a one-year-old, unblemished male lamb. They were then instructed to live with their lamb for three days as a household pet. Then, on the fourth day, that lamb was to be slaughtered in a way that did not involve breaking any bones. It is important to know that when Jesus was on the cross, Passover (to begin at sundown) was rapidly approaching. The guards wanted to expedite Jesus's death and decided to break his leg bones, because it would be harder for Jesus to breathe, and it would speed up his death. Had the guards broken his legs, Jesus could *not* have been described throughout history as "the Perfect Paschal Sacrifice"; it would have broken a rule of Passover preparation.

When the guards set out to break his legs, they realized he was already dead so they did *not* have to break his legs. Instead, they pierced his side and saw that water came out instead of blood because, when you die, the blood and water of your body gets separated, proving he had already died. He remained a perfect sacrifice that a violation of Jewish law (broken bones) did not negate. If Jesus's bones had been broken, his role as the Messiah would have made him "null and void" as a "Perfect" Paschal Sacrifice, disqualifying his body and blood from transforming sins from dirty to free and forgiven.

Jesus was God's plan for us ever since Plan A failed. Jesus is known to biblical scholars as the second Adam because the first Adam fell short of God's plan by falling victim to sin. Jesus came into this world because God wanted a better plan for us. All of those rules and remedies written out by Moses through communication with God stated in Leviticus did not work for God's chosen people. His "chosen" fell short every time and fell victim to sin.

The one thing God cannot do is coexist with sin in his eternal home. It cannot happen. Just like oil and water can't mix, God and sin cannot be combined either. Lucky for us, he so loved the world that he gave his only son up to be sacrificed so he could, through his blood, become every sin known to man. And thus *we* (his believers) could be purged from every sin known to man (John 3:16). Through our belief in him, our sins can be cleansed as well. Through Jesus's blood, we are forgiven, redeemed, and found blameless—unblemished like that Perfect Paschal Sacrifice. What a beautiful gift from God.

Evidence that increased my faith was learning that the prophet Isaiah predicted that the son of man would be conceived by a virgin and born in a stable (hence earning the title "Lamb of God"). The king of salvation born in a stable where asses defecate? What irony! But the ultimate sign of humility was always Jesus's message, which was synonymous with his humiliating death on a cross.

I learned another fact through my Christian Bible studies that, for Christians, validates that Jesus really is the son of God: Remember the tabernacle I spoke about? The part of the Jewish Temple that contained the altar where the blood of the animal sacrifices was offered? Only "high" priests were qualified to execute these burnt and guilt offerings in the tabernacle *behind* a curtain. The curtain or veil is called a brocade or *parocheth* in Hebrew. This curtain separated the Holy of Holies from the lesser holy places of the tabernacle. When Jesus took his last breath, that curtain ripped from top to bottom, symbolizing that no longer was it only high priests who had direct access to God. Now *anyone* had direct access through the blood of Christ. This is the belief that Jesus Christ was the ultimate, most worthy sacrifice to be the atonement for all—for every sin known to man, from smallest to biggest.

What a welcome improvement! Forgiveness had shifted from a deeply complicated process that we often got wrong, which often nullified the request to be forgiven, to an easy-peasy process of *grace*.

Grace

Grace cannot be earned. We thank God for that statement because we all fall short of deserving his perfect kingdom. We proved that in the Garden of Eden, when we only had one rule to follow and obey and we *failed*. As Christians, followers of Christ are forgiven through believing that Jesus Christ is God's Son, who was born in this life, through the virgin birth of Mary, the mother of God. He became the ultimate sacrifice for all of mankind who believe in him; he became every sin known to man, suffered a grueling death, and rose from the dead on the third day in fulfillment of the scriptures (God's word).

The illustration included here is compliments of my son Tommy, who summarized the basic concept of Christianity.

THE PROBLEM

The problem is that God cannot be where sin exists. Since the greatest among us is still guilty from sin, separation from God still exists.

Through the belief that Jesus's blood is redemptive, we are forgiven and found blameless. In God's mercy, through Grace, our sins are wiped away. We are now "worthy" to enter his kingdom.

THE SOLUTION

Symbolically, this happens the minute we accept Jesus as our "Lord and Savior"

Chapter 4

Bible 101, New Testament

The purpose of the New Testament was to outline Jesus's birth, life and preparation to submit himself to his Holy Father's will and be crucified so he could be the scapegoat for countless sinful people. The New Testament goes further, outlining the building of God's kingdom here on earth after the death of Jesus.

The New Testament has five major authors. One was Matthew, a tax collector who was an original apostle who traveled with Jesus as a follower and firsthand friend. His first hand written account is presented as the first book of the New Testament entitled, *The Gospel of Matthew.* Tax collectors were despised back in that day and viewed as among the lowest form of human life. Jesus elevates him by accepting him despite popular opinion.

Mark wrote his Gospel of the New Testament in about three and a half years. Mark's written account is the shortest of the four gospels and portrays Jesus as a "Servant of the People." Mark was the traveling companion of Paul and Barnabas when they traveled throughout Italy, Macedonia, Greece, Galatia and Carinthia spreading Christianity.

Luke was a physician and wrote in the most detail about Jesus's historical life. Luke's Gospel is the third book as it appears in the New Testament. It took him thirty-eight years to write this history. Luke wrote Acts as well, which was an account of the works of Jesus's friends/disciples who set out to build Christianity after Jesus was raised from the dead on that third day.

The fourth book of the New Testament was written by John the Apostle, who wrote two other books, John 1 and John 2. He also wrote the Book of Revelation, which details how this world will eventually end. John is described as "the One whom Jesus Loved." He knew Jesus personally and described in the most detail the miracles Jesus performed during the thirty-three years of his short life.

These four authors are the only writers of the entire New Testament whose testimonies carry direct quotes from Jesus. They each bring a different "spin" on Jesus's life. But they *all* agree and emphasize that his sole purpose for being born was to save mankind once and for all from their sins—his divine blood and sacrificial death offer eternal life for all who accept him as their personal Lord and Savior.

The fifth author of the New Testament is Paul, and he is of real importance to the Christian message. Paul never knew Jesus during his life. Paul got *very* acquainted with Jesus after his resurrection. Paul's original name was Saul. Saul first appears in chapter 9 of Acts. He is a Pharisee, which is under the umbrella of Judaism. the Pharisees followed the Jewish law precisely. Saul was greatly feared by Jesus's followers because he used to torture and kill Christians. In Acts 9, Saul is headed for Damascus with the intent of persecuting more Christians when he is suddenly knocked to the ground from the saddle of his horse.

We read in Acts 9:3–20 (ESV), "As he [Saul] was nearing Damascus [on his mission of persecution], suddenly, a brilliant light from heaven spotted down upon him! He fell to the ground and heard a voice saying to him, 'Saul! Saul! Why you persecuting me?' 'Who are you, Lord?' Paul asked. And the voice replied, 'I am Jesus, whom you are persecuting! but rise and enter the city and you will be told what you are to do.'"

The men who were traveling with Paul stood speechless with surprise, for they too witnessed the sound of someone's voice but saw no one. As Paul picked himself off the ground, he found that he was blind. God then told Saul that his new Christian name would be Paul from Tarsus and to await further instructions in the city of Damascus. There, Paul awaited further instructions from the Lord and remained there blinded.

In the meantime, God, through a dream, communicated to Ananias [a Christian] where he could find a blind Paul of Tarsus. God said, "Go over to Straight Street to the House of Judas. When you get there, ask for a man from Tarsus named Saul. He is praying to me right now. I have shown him a vision of a man named Ananias coming in and laying hands on him so he can see again" (Acts 9:11–12, NLT).

Ananias told God that Paul persecuted Christians and he was too afraid to do what God had asked. God then assured Ananias, "Go! This man is my chosen instrument to proclaim my name to the Gentiles and their kings, and to the people of Israel. I will show him how much he must suffer for my name" (Acts 9:15, NIV).

Friends, it is essential that you understand this part of the Bible. Ananias went as instructed. And the minute he touched Paul, the scales fell from his eyes. Paul then rested up and ate for three days. He then traveled the western regions for the next two decades, establishing the new Christian religion. He was persecuted, tortured, and jailed many times along the way. While in captivity, he wrote letters as follow-ups to all his beloved Christian followers. He miraculously escaped a few times with the help of Christians who had grown to love, admire, and trust him.

The letters of Paul are very inspiring and consist of the Letters of Paul to the Romans, Corinthians, Galatians, Ephesians, Colossians, Thessalonians, Timothy, Titus, Philemon, and the Hebrews.

I urge you to buy a Bible that is easy to understand and read these letters. They intimately talk about how to be a follower of Christ and Paul, through communication with Jesus and the Father, further explaining how loved we are by God and the rewards that await us in heaven. Paul had a great and intimate relationship with new Christians as they converted from Judaism to Christianity and sought his guidance along the way.

The book of Acts is very inspiring to me. Jesus's disciples were told to go out into the world and spread the "Good News" to anyone and everyone. But they were afraid, because the government would arrest and crucify anyone for contradicting Judaism, which was a religion of rules and remedies for broken rules. And introducing Christianity, a new religion offering unearned grace and the requirement to love God and each other to qualify for eternal life. These new followers were scared to death to contradict the strict rules of Judaism and remained in hiding until the Pentecost, which Christ spoke of before his death.

During Pentecost, the Holy Spirit was injected into the disciples in hiding. This 'Holy Spirit' empowered them and gave them purpose, conviction, and the confidence necessary to spread the Good News to the people under a government that was hostile to the Christian message. Jesus proved to the disciples that he was their Lord and Savior; and any sin they upheld would be upheld, and any sin they forgave would be forgiven. From Pentecost on, the disciples went out preaching the Good News and preaching God's word without fear of brutal persecution which was death on the cross.

Finally, it is essential to have knowledge of the miracles that took place, performed by Jesus when he ministered to his followers in the four Gospels—Matthew, Mark, Luke, and John.

Jesus was crucified at the age of thirty-three. When he was an infant, God sent the holy family from Bethlehem to Egypt because King Herod, the then king of Israel, had ordered the slaughter of all male children under the age of two. He had done so because prophecy dictated that a future "King of the Jews" would be born. The paranoid Herod understood this infant to be a future threat to his authority.

The Three Wise Men set out to find this future king at birth, bearing precious gifts of gold, frankincense, and myrrh. Herod asked them upon their return to reveal the route they had taken to find this holy baby. They were advised by God, through a dream, not to return the way they had come and not to honor the king's request to reveal Jesus's location. The Three Wise Men obeyed God's instructions. God was protecting Jesus from harm so he could carry out God's Plan B for the well-being of mankind.

The very first miracle Jesus performed was at a wedding. Weddings at that time were celebrated for days. At this particular wedding, the hosts ran out of wine. Mary knew what Jesus was capable of, so she ordered the servants to bring barrels of water to Jesus. Jesus was annoyed, because he believed that the time of miracles had not yet come. But he honored his mother's request and changed the water into wine (John 2:1–11).

Jesus touched a leper, and he was instantly healed (Matthew 8:1–4).

A Roman Army captain asked Jesus to heal his servant's son, who was paralyzed and racked with pain. Jesus offered to go to the captain's house. But the captain replied, "I do not deserve to have you come under my roof. But just say the word, and my servant shall be healed." Jesus stood amazed at the soldier's faith, and Jesus said to the Roman captain, "Go—Let it be done just as you believed it would." The boy was healed at that moment (Matthew 8:5–13, NIV).

When Jesus arrived at Peter's house, he found Peter's mother-in-law to be sick with a high fever. When Jesus touched her hand, the fever left her (Matthew 8:14–15).

Several demon-possessed people were brought to Jesus. And when Jesus spoke one word, all of the demons fled, and all of the sick were healed. This also fulfilled the prophecy of Isaiah, which stated, "He took our infirmities and bore our diseases" (Matthew 8:16–17, NIV).

In Matthew 8:23–32 (NIV), Jesus fell asleep in a boat with his disciples. The entire boat started violently rocking as a storm was brewing and waves were high. We read this:

The disciples woke Jesus, saying, "Lord, save us, we are going to drown!" Jesus replied, "You of little faith, why are you so afraid?" Then he got up, rebuked the wind and waves and the sea was completely calm. The men were amazed and asked, "What kind of a man is this? Even the winds and the waves obey him!" When they reached land, more people came to meet Jesus who were possessed by demons. The men started shouting, "What do you want with us,

Son of God? Have you come here to torment us before the appointed time?" Some distance from them Jesus saw a herd of pigs feeding in the distance. The demons begged Jesus, "If you drive us out, send us into the herd of pigs."

He said to them, "Go!" So, they came out and went into the pigs. Then the whole herd rushed down the steep bank into the lake and died in the waters below.

Jesus continued healing the sick, paralyzed, and blind as described in Matthew 9:1–38. And Mark chapters 1 through five 5 outline many miracles of healing, resurrecting the dead, and casting out demons.

One of Jesus's most famous miracles is explained in Mark 6:38–45. Jesus ministered to a crowd of five thousand and realized that the crowd needed to eat. He took the food he had between himself and his disciples, totaling five fish and two loaves of bread. Jesus looked up to heaven, gave thanks for the food and started breaking up the fish and bread to place before the people. The crowd ate until they were filled. After all five thousand men and children ate, the scraps were collected, and twelve baskets of scraps were collected!

Mark continues explaining Jesus's teachings and miracles of healings well into chapter 15.

All four gospels outline Jesus's death and resurrection and the many miracles that Jesus performed before and after his death. Another very famous miracle was when Jesus raised his cousin Lazarus from the dead, four days after his death and entombment, but not before mourning his death and crying (John 11:1–44).

How comforting it has always been to me that Jesus understands the anguish and grief of losing someone you love. I have gone to him many times with my grief, asking him for comfort.

Chapter 5

Nothing Can Separate Us from the Love of God

After Jesus died on the cross, his loved ones prepared Jesus's body for burial. It was to be the Sabbath come sundown on Friday. And until the following sundown on Saturday, the Jewish laws forbade any work. He was destined for a poor man's grave, but God inspired a rich landowner named Joseph of Arimathea to take total care of Jesus after his death and permitted Jesus to use space in his grave cave. The Roman government ordered that a massive stone be placed, covering the tomb's entrance. They ordered two soldiers to guard the tomb; it was feared that someone would steal the body, giving credit to the rumor that Jesus would rise from the dead.

What happens next is found in Matthew 28:1–18 (NLT):

Early on Sunday morning, as the new day was dawning, Mary Magdalene and the other Mary went out to the tomb. Suddenly there was a great earthquake; for an angel of the Lord came down from heaven and rolled aside the stone and sat on it. His face Shone like lightning and his clothing was a brilliant white. The guards shook with fear when they saw him, and fell into a dead faint. Then the angel spoke to the women, "Don't be frightened!" He said "I know you are looking for Jesus who was crucified, but he isn't here! For he has come back to life again just as he said he would. Come in and see where his body was laying …

"And now, go quickly and tell his disciples that he is risen from the dead, and that he is going to Galilee to meet them there. That is my message to them."

The women ran from the tomb, badly frightened, but also filled with joy, rushing to find the disciples to give them the Angel's message. As they went, Jesus met them and greeted them. As they ran to him, grasped his feet, and worshipped him. Then Jesus said to them, "Don't be afraid! Go tell my brothers to leave for Galilee, and they will see me there."

The Report of the Guard

As the women were on the way, some of the guards went into the city, some of the Temple Police who had been guarding the tomb went to the chief priests and told them what had happened. A meeting of all the Jewish leaders was called, and it was decided to bribe the police to say that they had all been asleep when Jesus's disciples came during the night and stole his body. If the governor hears about it, the council promised it will stand up for you and everything will be alright. So, the police accepted the bribe and said what they were told to. Their story spread widely among the Jews and it is still believed to this very day.

Then the eleven disciples left for Galilee, going to the mountain where Jesus had said they would find him. There they met him and worshiped him but some of them were not sure it was really Jesus. He told his disciples, "I have been given all authority in heaven and on Earth, therefore go and make disciples in all the nations, baptizing them into the name of the Father and the Son and the Holy Spirit and then teach these new disciples to obey all the commands I have given you from me: and be sure of this that I am with you always even to the end of the world."

Before Jesus was crucified, he tried to prepare his disciples for his death and told them that he would destroy the temple but rebuild it by rising on the third day. But they could not begin to grasp the concept. Then he tried to console them by stating that now, being alive, he could only be with them in person, but after his death and resurrection, he would be with them always. They could not understand that either. He meant spiritually—that once invited in, he could remain in their hearts.

They remained together but were very scared. The Romans were persecuting Christians and the disciples feared they would be next. Jesus appeared to his friends a few times and told them not to go out proclaiming the Good News around the world until the time was right, and he would let them know when.

The "when" was revealed to the disciples at Pentecost, when the Holy Spirit entered the upper room with a huge wind and empowered the disciples not to be afraid of persecution, that God would give them the perfect words and protection they needed to spread the Good News about Jesus: "God so loved the world that he gave his only son (to be born and crucified) so that anyone who believes in him shall not perish but have eternal life" (John 3:16, NIV).

After giving you this background, I think you can understand how blessed I am to be able to say that there is never a waking moment when God is not on my mind. As a Christian, once you accept Jesus as God's son who was born through the Virgin Mary to die for the sins of all and was raised from the dead on the third day, Jesus occupies a place in your heart from that day forth. And he promises that he will not separate from you.

In Romans 8:38–39 (NLT), Paul writes to the Roman Christians, "For I am convinced that nothing can ever separate us from his love—death can't, and life can't. The Angels won't, and all the powers of Hell itself cannot keep God's love away. Our fears for today, our worries about tomorrow, or where we are high above the sky, or in the deepest ocean oh, nothing will ever be able to separate us from the love of God demonstrated by our Lord Jesus Christ when he died for us."

I know this. But I am blessed because I am *always* thinking about him—*always*. When the neighbor shows up unexpectedly, I smile and greet him or her, but I am just thinking about Jesus. When I'm driving, I am thinking about Jesus. When I listen to Christian music, I am singing about Jesus. When I have a passenger in my car, I will be talking to him, her, or them and listening and contributing to our conversation, but I'm also thinking about Jesus. When I'm cooking—you guessed it—I am thinking about Jesus. When I have my second glass of wine, I am talking about Jesus and God's great love for us. Since Jesus Christ is always on my mind, I always feel joy in my heart. And for this, I am deeply grateful.

Like you, I always use my eyes while awake, but I never think about them. Like you, I always use my nose when I breathe, but I never think about my nose until I sneeze; and then I'm *still* not thinking about my nose. I'm thinking about the tissue I need! But God is always with me, and I feel like I am always with him. One couldn't ask for a bigger or better blessing than that.

I also believe that anyone can develop this kind of relationship with their God. All they need to do is pray for a better relationship with him with a *humble* heart. Ask God not what he can do for *you* but, rather, ask what you can do for God. Ask God to reveal himself to you. Then go forth with an open mind and an open heart. But prepare to be *amazed*.

He will put people in your path that need your help. By helping that person, you will be serving God, and it feels fantastic. I don't mean that he will put someone in your path whose "help" requires you to spend a lot of money or to jeopardize your safety. You may see someone who looks lost. Ask the person if he or she needs help. You may see an elderly person struggling to open a door. Stop what you are doing and jump to the person's aid. When you are in line at a drive-through coffee place, tell the attendant you want to pay for the coffee of the person behind you. Give someone who looks sad a compliment. You may be very surprised at how great you feel afterward; I believe that these "feel-good" emotions are God's way of showing his approval of the work you are doing on his behalf.

One of my favorite recollections of when God put someone directly in my path who needed help was on a beautiful, warm, sunny day in May 2008.

I was preparing to take my father for a quick visit to the doctor to have his blood taken. My children were all in school, and I had just returned from Sam's Club, where almost all the groceries I bought came in bulk size and double quantities. As I was putting away my groceries, there was a knock at the door.

That's strange, I thought to myself. I was not expecting anyone.

When I opened the door, I saw a mother with a young daughter, who I estimated to be no older than four. I immediately noticed the flimsy shoes they both were wearing. I said, "Hello. Can I help you?"

They only spoke Spanish, and when I realized that, I spoke to them in Spanish, and their relieved faces lit up like a Christmas tree. The mom explained to me that they didn't have money for a taxi, so she and her daughter walked to my neighborhood trying to find a preschool so they could register for summer classes.

I explained that the preschool was across the highway among the apartment buildings. I offered to take them there myself. I would then take my dad to the doctor's office as planned. We all got into my car, including Dad, who took the front passenger seat, and the mother and daughter took the back seat.

Within five minutes, they entered the school, and I said I would wait there for them. Two minutes later, the mom came out without the daughter to say that registration would take about an hour, and she did not want me to wait.

I told her, "This is perfect. I will take my father to his doctor's appointment and will come back for you two and will drive you home."

She was very appreciative, and we both went on our way.

When I came back for them, they were both ready and waiting for me. I asked the mom in Spanish, "Do you have food at home to feed your family?"

She said that she had some rice for tonight. She went on to say that ICE (Immigrations and Customs Enforcement) had arrested her husband and sent him back to Mexico, and they had no income. This had just happened two days ago. She also had an older son who was in school full-time.

Then I asked her in Spanish, "How many doors did you knock

on before mine?" At that time, there was no one who spoke Spanish who lived in my neighborhood, and I couldn't help but wonder how she had found my house.

The mom told me that I was the first house she had called on. My jaw dropped. I believed all the more now that God had sent her to me. I told her to come into my house. When she did, I went through my pantry and gave her half of everything I had just bought—bread, pasta, rice, soup, chicken, butter, cheese, cereal, eggs, pasta sauce, mac and cheese, you name it! Then I gave her a child's pillow and told her that her daughter would need a tiny pillow and a cozy blanket for naptime at the preschool.

She agreed and gratefully accepted both. I then got ready to drive the two of them back to their house. By then, my three children were home, and my oldest son went with us to help carry the groceries into her apartment.

As my car was being unloaded, I was given some time to inconspicuously observe this immigrants' neighborhood. I saw many adults out in the street or sitting on their porches. It was 3:00 p.m., but it seemed like the men weren't working but, rather, socializing. The houses were decrepit and neglected by the "slumlords" who owned them but rented them out at exorbitant prices. It was the kind of neighborhood you would only dare visit in the daytime.

What I knew was that Jesus had led the mom to my house, and I felt deeply honored. Jesus was entrusting me to help someone in need. He had faith that I would come through. He inspired me to go to Sam's that morning because he is a strategic planner. I was often low on food because we were a family of six if you include my dad, who lived with us for the last ten years of his life. At that time, I used to shop twice a week for food because we would go through it so fast. Jesus did not want his children to go hungry, so he made sure my pantry was overflowing before that mom knocked on my door.

You may be tempted to categorize this story as a simple "coincidence." Will your mind be changed if I tell you that my pastor explained through his Homily one Sunday morning that in the ancient language of Hebrew, there is no word for "coincidence" because everything good is planned and controlled by God. Therefore "coincidence" or, "by chance" is evaporated from their vocabulary.

I believe this is a great story, but it gets even better when you consider the issue of timing. This was a Monday morning. Just yesterday, my family and I had been in church, and the Gospel reading was exemplified through the mom and daughter who knocked on my door. See if you can recognize the similarities between the gospel message and my living experience with the Hispanic mom and her daughter.

The Gospel reading was from Matthew 25:31–40, NIV, on "The Sheep and the Goats":

When the son of man comes in his glory, and all the angels with him, he will sit on his glorious throne. All the nations will be gathered before him, and he will separate the people one from another as the shepherd separates the sheep from the goats. He will put the sheep on his right and the goats on his left.

Then the king will say to those on his right, "Come you who are blessed by my father; take your inheritance, the kingdom for you since the creation of the world. For I was hungry and you gave me something to eat, I was thirsty and you gave me something to drink, I was a stranger and you invited me in, I needed clothes and you clothed me; I was sick and you looked after me, I was in prison and you came to visit me."

Then the righteous will answer him, "Lord when did we see you hungry and feed you, or thirsty and give you something to drink? When did we see you as a stranger and invite you in, or needing clothes and clothe you? When did we see you sick or in prison and go to visit you?"

The king will reply, "Truly I tell you, whatever you did for one of the least of these brothers and sisters of mine, you did for me."

There was a song I used to sing as a child that I learned in church, and it was based on this chapter, Matthew 25. I didn't know what the Gospel was back then, but the song motivated me at a very young age to do nice things for other people, because when you make someone else happy, you make God happy. The name of the song is "Whatsoever You Do" by Willard F. Jabusch and Owen Alstott. The refrain is, "Whatsoever you do, to the least of my people, that you do unto me." My favorite verse of the song sums up the Gospel of Matthew 25:31–40, "When I was thirsty you gave me to drink; when I was hungry you gave me to eat; now enter into the home of my father"

The converse is also true. When you treat someone poorly, you are offending God because he loves that person you are gossiping about or conspiring against or cheating or robbing or physically or emotionally abusing. When you hurt someone else, you are also offending God.

The New Testament gives lessons in how to be humble, as humility is a righteous trait admired and loved by God. There are seventy-three verses explaining the benefits of being humble in the Bible. With humbleness comes understanding, wisdom, and exaltation. Pride and arrogance are the opposite, and their effects against man are spoken of very seriously in the Old and New Testaments. Arrogance and pride hinder our intimacy with God and love for others. We need to forsake pride and embrace humility.

C.S. Lewis states, "According to Christian Teachers, Pride is of the utmost evil, along with unchastity, anger, greed, drunkenness. It was through pride that the Arc Angel Lucifer became the Devil. Pride leads to every other vice; It is the complete anti-God state of mind. It is Satan's most effective & destructive tool." This is clearly stated and taught all throughout the Bible for our benefit.

Do you know what happens to many people when they are amazed at the numerous times they see evidence of God working in their lives? They want to give back to God by living the way God wants them to live. God's demands are so simple. He wants us to love him with all our hearts, and he wants us to love our neighbor as we love ourselves. Once we do this, the world becomes a better place. The better place begins in our hearts. We become more at peace. Our anxieties lessen, and our spirit's soar. Jesus knew that the most important commandment of all was to love your neighbor. Treat others like you yourself want to be treated; then Matthew's gospel of the sheep and the goats falls into place.

In Matthew, "Legal experts of the Sadducees and Pharisees tried to trick Jesus by asking him, 'Teacher, what is the greatest commandment in the Law?'" (Matthew 22:36, NIV).

There were 613 laws that Jews were required to obey.

The passage continues, "Jesus replied, "You must love the Lord your God with all your heart, with all your soul, with all your mind. This is the first and greatest commandment. And the second is like it: You must love your neighbor as yourself. All the Law and the Prophets hang on these two commands'" (Matthew 22:37–40, NIV).

I remember hearing this reading in church when I was seventeen. Believe it or not, this reading made me very sad. I said to myself, "Jeanine! How can this be? I know that I do love my neighbor as myself. I have always treated people like I myself want to be treated. That part was easy. But that first most important commandment to *love God* deeply—I come up empty-hearted! How can that be? I have spent every week of my life in church. I can honestly say that I believe wholeheartedly that he exists, so my faith is strong. I respect God and fear him, but I am empty and numb to the *love* part. I am alarmed! I do not feel love for God! He is not personal to me, and I don't feel an intimacy toward him."

At seventeen, I was really disturbed. I am not able to relate to or participate in *the most important requirement of Christianity*! I decided to think of a solution. I said, "Dear Lord, I want to obey you, and I want to grow in my faith. Please teach me how to love you."

From that day forward, He has helped me do just that. He gave me a desire to study the bible. He taught me that our God is a personal God who wants an intimate relationship with each and every one of us. I think many people stay away from studying the Bible because they assume that a book that is thousands of years old cannot apply to our present lives.

I have studied it and relied on it for the last thirty years, and I hope you will come to understand that it is just as relevant today as it was thousands of years ago. It understands human nature, and it teaches you how to live your best life. Also, the New Testament is like a love letter from God to us! The more I studied and read the Bible, the stronger my love has become for God.

He has more than answered my call for help in learning to love God with all my heart, mind, body, and soul. He will answer your calls for help as well. All you need to do is earnestly ask and prepare yourselves for great discoveries and future amazements. I recommend that you start documenting on the notepad app from your cell phone so that you may write down little things you notice that call your attention to God. Always have tools "at the ready" to jot down ways he might have communicated with you throughout the day. Make it your business to notice the little things.

Consider a few examples:

- Did the perfect song come on the radio at the perfect time with a message that answers a prayer or a concern that has been preoccupying your thoughts?
- When you were running late at the grocery store, did someone shorten the line for you by insisting you go first?
- Did a previously scheduled appointment get canceled when you needed extra time to study?
- Did someone appear out of nowhere to help you when you needed it?

Chapter 6

November 23, 2001

I will never forget the details of this day. The day before had been amazing. It was Thanksgiving, and I had entertained my side of the family. My two nephews were up with their girlfriends, my brother and sister-in-law were there, along with my father, who lived with us, and my twin sister, Francine. We had such a great day. My three children at the time were seven, six, and three. There was so much holiday magic in the air, and it felt good.

The nation was still in mourning after 9/11/2001, and I was tired of being heavyhearted and sad. I had great energy that day. I had spent that week preparing all of the traditional Thanksgiving recipes with all the trimmings. The dinner table was beautifully set with my fine Lenox China and Noritake crystal. My heart was full, grateful, and intensely mindful of the thousands of families who were brokenhearted because their loved one went to work like countless times before, only, this one time, did not return. The pain was still raw, and millions of American flags were still displayed at half-staff, representing the wounds of a nation that would never be quite the same again.

Somehow, my gratitude overpowered my heavy heart and I was able to fully celebrate my favorite holiday with my loved ones present. I had so much energy that day that I insisted on washing all the dishes and taking our small crowd of guests around the block to burn off some carbs and make room for dessert. I proudly led them around our neighborhood's biggest circle, announcing that our immediate family knew every person living in every house. I showed my family the location of our annual block party and the fact that every home in my neighborhood was privately designed and unique to it's owner. At that time, we were one of the youngest families on the block that had children. What a great place that was to be in life—young, successful, and healthy. Life was better than good. And it humbled me because, while I have always worked my hardest to achieve, I did not deserve a quality of life any greater than the hard worker who was rolling his sleeves up next to me or those in neighboring cities or states or even neighboring countries.

In the United States, the day after Thanksgiving is always referred to as Black Friday. Little did I know how *dark* this particular Friday would become. The day, for me, had started out slowly. I cooked a big breakfast for the entire family and then went downstairs in the basement to do my aerobic workout. I was very much in shape. I was very thin, so I only worked out three days a week, but it kept me strong and my stamina long.

After my workout, I felt like a sparkling diamond. I was exceedingly happy! My endorphins had kicked in from the workout. As I took my post-workout shower, I quickly reminded myself that I had to be at the funeral parlor by 2:30 p.m. One of my dear colleagues had just lost her mom after a long battle with cancer. My colleague and I had bonded over her experiences with her sick mom because my mom had also died of cancer. I knew all too personally the emotional ups and downs of the journey. The World Language Department of my school planned on meeting as a group at the funeral parlor by 2:30. My daughter, who never wanted me to leave the house, begged and cried for me not to go. I reassured her I would be back in an hour, and I would be "all yours."

I'd gotten in my car to leave when my husband called me out of the car. He wanted me to check out some carpet he had just bought from Home Depot. I got out of the car. But I was losing my patience. All I wanted to do was leave so I could get back. I was on top of the world.

When I got back into my car and started backing out of my driveway, I got an eerie chill that went down my spine. I was reminded of how I felt every time I made a right turn. For at least six weeks now, I had this weird premonition that something airborne was going to hit the roof of my car. Frequently, just during the last couple of months, when I made a right turn, I would get a weird chill powerful enough to cause me to shiver while making a right turn. The hairs on my neck would stand on end for just a second or two, and then it was over.

As I approached the neighborhood traffic light, I noticed to my left that there was no approaching traffic. I was able to do something I rarely could. I made a right on red, which was allowed at that time. As soon as I got on highway 18S, I became alarmed as I noticed a very low car approaching me from the other side of the highway. This very low-to-the-ground red Toyota was coming right for me!

I tried to get out of the car's path by hugging the car in front of me as an attempt to get around the car or to get the driver to speed up so I might avoid an accident. The driver in front of me was not vigilant enough to see what was happening behind him. I remember thinking that the driver approaching me must be dead; he must have had a heart attack or a brain aneurysm. He was driving very slowly. As soon as the Toyota driver T-boned the back of my passenger door, I became acutely aware that my SUV was going to flip. This horrified me because I was always afraid to flip. I never even went on those adventurous roller-coaster rides that would turn you upside down—simply because I didn't want to go upside down! I was undeniably aware that I had no choice in the matter. I was flipping.

The second I flipped I realized I could not move my legs. I had my seatbelt on, so I was literally upside down in my driver's seat. I heard a door close behind me and footsteps approaching my car, and all I could say was "Help me!"

I thought I was shouting, but I could hardly hear myself. I remember saying, "I can't move my legs—pray for me. I can't move my legs."

Without warning, two men, a police officer, who knew how to

proceed with caution, and my husband and it was utmost caution that they demonstrated. Before I knew it, the ambulance came, and the EMTs put me on a backboard and stabilized my back and neck. My body must have been in shock because I wasn't panicking or in pain. I was very hopeful that the hospital would make everything right again.

When I got to the hospital, a whole team of trauma experts descended upon me and swarmed around me as if I was their first priority. I remember them cutting my clothes off and sending me into the CT scan room. After the CT scan, my husband met me on the way to the MRI. After the MRI, my husband and a priest, a dear friend of the family, were by my side. Fr. Jim was the principal of the Catholic school directly across the street from the hospital, at the time of the accident. My principal, my mother-in-law and Fr. Jim had all taught together for over thirty years, and were great friends. My principal had just retired and moved to Florida. My in-laws, Blanquita and Carl, had been visiting with her in Florida when my husband, Tom, called her with news of the accident. The family priest, Father Jim, had sprung into action, and he held my hand every minute.

The doctor came out and told me I had broken my neck. I knew two other men in town who had broken their necks as well, and they were both quadriplegics. I remember asking the doctor, "What are you saying—that I am going to be confined to a wheelchair for the rest of my life?"

The doctor ever so slightly nodded. It was such a slight movement I wasn't even sure he had nodded at all. But I remember that I shouted, "Noooooooo!" and I began to cry.

How could I not move my legs? I had just done an intense and very strenuous aerobic workout in my basement. Yesterday, I had hosted over fifteen people for Thanksgiving dinner! The day before that, I had prepared homemade Puerto Rican rice and beans and chicken and rice for Steven and Marisa's school in celebration of Thanksgiving. Just last Sunday, I was teaching religious education to St. Matthias's CCD Students. The Friday before that, Steven and Marisa were helping me cook and serve meals at our local soup kitchen, Elijah's Promise. Never a spare minute was idle but, rather, filled with something meaningful. And my job! I taught Spanish to high school students! It was only November! How would I ever be able to teach again? How could I not walk? *This can't be happening to me!* All of these thoughts raced through my head until I heard a voice call me back.

"Let's pray," Father Jim said. He started praying, and I shut my mouth. All good Christian girls keep quiet when they hear prayers.

But my thoughts were racing. The first thing you think is "no way," as in *this can't be happening to me,* "no way" as in *they are not going to tell me I can't walk.* The denial runs deep.

I told Tom that if it was not for our children, I would rather die, because he did not sign up for this injury. He said, "yes I did, for better or worse, in sickness and in health, until…"

The team of doctors asked me to raise my right arm, and I couldn't. The ER Nurse raised my right hand for me and told me to hold my arm up, and I couldn't. My arm dropped to my side like a lead balloon.

After my six-hour neck fusion surgery, I learned that the man behind the wheel had fallen asleep. Aside from that, I don't remember our conversation. I underwent neck fusion surgery because my neck needed to be stabilized using some bone taken from my hip along with skillfully placed plates and bolts.

I did not realize I was alive until seven days later. It was my thirty-seventh birthday. I remember waking up in the ICU with all of Tom's relatives around me and my father holding my hand. I woke up seeing the worried looks on their faces, but it never occurred to me that I could have died.

Tom was about to bring the kids in to see me. The hospital had a program for families of the catastrophically injured. The kids were in a separate room meeting with a nurse, learning that they were going to see me in a neck brace and with all kinds of tubes coming out of me. The emphasis was that there was nothing to fear. Again, my kids were three, six and seven, and they needed their mommy.

When the kids came in to see me, they were still upset. I told them how much I loved them and that everything was going to be OK. My oxygen level started to drop, and my medical team recommended that I get intubated, so the kids had a very rushed visit with me, and they were made to leave before they were ready to do so. My three children left crying, and my heart was broken. I remained intubated and, for the next three weeks, would remain in ICU.

After the first week, when I was intubated a second time, Tom was asked to leave the room because the doctors needed to work over me. Tom went to the balcony to pray. He was deeply worried I would never be able to breathe on my own without the help of a respirator. As he was praying, a tremendous sense of peace washed over him, and he felt assured by God that everything would be OK. He just needed to let go and trust God.

Within thirty seconds of this experience, Tom's cell phone rang. It was his sister Terry who lived in Tampa. She had just gotten home from visiting us and helping with the kids. "Tom," she said in an excited voice, I know that Jeanine is going to be OK!"

Tom wanted to know why she had come to that conclusion. "How do you know?" he asked eagerly.

Terry continued, "I was driving and decided to turn off the radio and pray. Suddenly, I felt this overwhelming sense of peace rush through me from head to toe, and I just knew right then that Jeanine is going to be fine."

Tom felt very hopeful because Terry explained exactly what had just happened to him, validating for Tom that the peace that had washed over him was real and could be trusted. When Tom explained to his sister that the same thing happened to him, that this intense wave of peace had washed over him just as she had described, they rejoiced and thanked God for answering their prayers and relieving their hearts.

I was getting transferred to the best rehabilitation hospital on the East Coast. At that time, Kessler Institute for Rehabilitation ranked second in the entire country, and I couldn't wait. I wanted to be proactive in my recovery. I was not getting any stronger lying flat on my back in this bed. I needed to get to rehab so I could build my strength and begin my journey toward self-improvement.

Unfortunately, I developed pneumonia at the hospital, and Kessler Institute for Rehabilitation would not take a patient with pneumonia or a fever. I could not eat or drink anything either because my doctors were afraid the food would go into my lungs, and I would aspirate. I felt desperately thirsty and would salivate at the thought of a cold gallon of spring water that was sweating on the outside waiting for me to open it and chug it, offering relief to my intense thirst. My medical team assured me my IV was delivering all the liquid my body needed and I was not clinically thirsty. To this day, almost twenty-two years later, I still remember the magnitude of the thirst I experienced and still believe I suffered from that thirst and it was real. I was fed Ensure through a stomach tube and never felt "hungry." But the "thirst" I felt tormented me and overwhelmed my senses.

Despite this intense sensation of thirst, my spirits remained high. I put a lot of hope into my thoughts of rehabilitation. I was in great shape and wanted to be proactive in my recovery. The ICU nurses were extraordinary. In fact, I remain friends with two to this day. They washed my hair and bathed me every day, and for that, I was deeply grateful. One of the night nurses made a cheerful-colored hospital gown for me. She wanted me to look great when my children came to visit me! Another made me a recording of upbeat 80's music to play during the day. These trauma nurses were very special people, and I will never forget and will forever appreciate the dedicated service and compassion they bestowed on me.

One day as Tom was beside my bed for a visit, his cell phone rang. It was a friend and former colleague offering Tom a better-paying job in a field that fell under the broad category of civil engineering. Land remediation was a field that was very foreign to my husband, who used to work for Mark. Mark had always appreciated Tom's extraordinary intelligence, coupled with his loyalty to his employers and his strong work ethic. The point I want to make is that Tom had no experience in this field. Mark made it clear to Tom that this job was missing a project manager and that he would be the perfect addition to his team. This new job offered a big increase in pay, more vacation time, and very improved benefits. Despite Tom having no prior experience, we both knew this opportunity was blessed by God and provided by divine intervention.

As it turned out, the increase in salary matched the amount of money I had been making as a part-time teacher! I always had to work, and we lived paycheck to paycheck. Now that I could not work, God was providing more money for us—nothing more than what we needed yet nothing less. Little did I know, this was just the first of many interventions my God was going to provide for me.

Jesus explains to us through scripture, Matthew 6:26 (NIV), "Look at the birds in the air; they do not sow or reap or gather into barns, and yet your heavenly Father feeds them. Are you not of more value than they?"

The next intervention was right around the corner. I became very discouraged because, every night in the middle of the night, I would spike a fever. And this fever was what was preventing my admittance into Kessler. That next night, before Tom left my bedside, he prayed over me, asking that God eliminate my pneumonia, as well as my high fever so I may go to Kessler as soon as tomorrow. That night, my fever did not return; nor did my pneumonia. And I was on my way to Kessler—a step on which I had placed high hopes for a major recovery.

I arrived at Kessler on December 16, three and a half weeks after my accident. I met my new doctors, nurses, and physical therapists. The protocol then was that each patient receives ninety minutes of physical therapy a day and ninety minutes of occupational therapy a day. I asked for an additional hour of therapy in the workout room. They were quick to accommodate my request, so I had four hours of exercise every day to try and make my body strong again.

I had ups and downs but mostly high hopes for my future. I had a beautiful family; a wonderful, loving, and dedicated husband; and affectionate children who showered me with love. You know what they say about love; it conquers all. Bill Devaux, a contributing writer for Crosswalk.com explains:

It is often said that love conquers all, that love is the greatest force in the universe. It is the force that gives healing and life, binds souls together, and whispers to us that all will be well. If we let the radiance of love beckon us back to its source, we find that there is a Lover behind love, and that Lover is committed to conquering all that is not love and all that is not lovely.

That Lover is God Himself, the Father, Son and Holy Spirit, whose life together is always one of mutual love. Love conquers all because God is Love and love has already won.

Chapter 7

My Journey toward Healing

On the home front, I was blown away when I found out what my neighbors were planning. They all got together and made a schedule. Every day about dinnertime, a beautiful, hot homemade meal was delivered to my house for my family. What a relief to me! My family did not have to worry about getting fed. An unintentional helpful side effect of this generosity was that Tom did not have to go grocery shopping. He only had to run to the nearest gas station to buy bread, eggs, and milk—just the basic breakfast essentials. Nobody knew how much Tom hated grocery shopping more than I did. My Dewey Heights family was fulfilling the most important first commandment. Jesus said, in Matthew 22:37–38 (NLT), "You should love the Lord your God with all your heart, all your soul and all your mind and love your neighbor as you would yourself." And love me they did!

Another blessing was that after over forty years of teaching, my mother-in-law had just retired. My in-laws lived right across the street. Blanquita was able to put my kids on the bus every day after giving them breakfast. Tom had a new job and had to leave very early in the morning. The confidence I had that my family was well cared for was priceless. The peace of mind that came with this additional blessing allowed me to concentrate on just me, myself, and I so I could return home as quickly as possible.

During rehab, I learned how to transfer myself from the

wheelchair onto the exercise mat, stretch myself, and do exercises involving my upper body. Because I was paralyzed from the chest down, these tasks were monumental.

When paralysis occurs, losses are great, and one needs time to grieve. The losses are too traumatic to understand all at once. Every day needs to be taken one at a time. Besides the lack of mobility, everyday function of the bowels and bladder are lost. They are paralyzed as well, and classes were needed to teach me how to care for my body going forward. There was much to learn and much to do.

My psychiatrist gave me day passes to go home on Saturdays and Sundays so I could see my children, which was another blessing to count. I could not stay home overnight for insurance reasons. I had to return to Kessler every night of each weekend, but the weekends were very precious to me. I got to see my children. I did not want to stay home overnight because there were too many things I could not do on my own, such as dressing and showering myself. Sunday nights were very tough on me and my children, because we knew we would not see each other again for six whole days until the next Saturday. I tried to hold it together for the benefit of my children. The truth is, that as soon as I got transferred into the car, I would cry half of the way back to Kessler in anticipation of how much I would miss my babies until I could see them again.

Sometimes, when the 3:00 p.m. hour came, my heart would start to throb because I missed my children so much. At 3:00 p.m. every school day afternoon, the second half of the day would start. I would get my three children off the bus, fix them a snack, and help them all at the kitchen table with their homework. It was a very special time of the day, when I felt that no one could take my place. While at Kessler, I managed to call them every morning before their bus came. I made sure to tell them how much I love them and to wish them a great day.

Overall, my spirits remained high at Kessler because during my stay most of the in-patients who had just suffered a spinal cord injury were much worse off than I was. I was not grateful for their more unfortunate situation—I just had no problem seeing my blessings.

For example, if the damage to my spinal cord had been a fraction higher than it was, the strength and ability to use of my arms would have been impeded and greatly compromised. I had my two arms and one hand. A lot of patients had a higher neck injury than mine, and the results were very much worse. Many patients could not move their arms at all or even shrug their shoulders.

Think about that for a moment. Many actions that we take for granted would now be impossible. What happens when your nose itches? Without arm movement, you are unable to scratch it. Come to think of it, what about when *anything* itches? Without the use of your arms, nothing gets scratched. What about eating? Being paralyzed, you still get hungry, but without arm movement, you cannot feed yourself. What about when you sneeze and need a tissue? Someone else must help you wipe your nose. What about when your phone rings? You can talk, but you cannot answer your phone. When you see a loved one, they hug you, but you are not able to return one to them. How does one operate a wheelchair? Or steer one?

Fortunately, there is a way. Victims of high-level injuries can blow through a steel straw that controls the power chair. A steady stream of air versus small puffs, along with personally designed patterns of air and the way it is blown through a straw, steers the wheelchair. I have also seen skilled wheelchair drivers use their chins over a ball similar to a roll-on deodorant device that can steer a chair straight, to the right, left, and so on. Many of these advanced chairs have a driving and steering mechanism on the back of their wheelchair, making it easy for a caregiver to take over and steer in order to relieve the driver.

I thought I was much too young to be in a wheelchair. I soon found out that, statistically speaking, thirty-seven is old to suffer a spinal cord injury. Typically, young men break their necks when they dive into a shallow pool or dive into a wave or jump from a high spot and fall. These self-inflicted injuries happen young—at seventeen, eighteen, or twenty-one years of age. Spinal cord injuries are very cruel; they happen in one second when you least expect it.

My mind and heart are at peace because I know that my car

accident was not my fault. I did not do anything on my end to cause this catastrophe to happen. What I did find out was that the driver who had hit me had fallen asleep behind the wheel at 2:08 p.m. and hit me at 2:09 p.m. My car was totaled, and so was I.

I thought of my students. They were without a teacher. I loved my job, and I had the perfect part-time schedule. My first class began at 9:30 a.m., and my last class ended at 12:30, just three hours a day. I taught two ninety-minute classes back-to-back. It was my intention to return to a full-time teaching schedule the next year, when my youngest son, Tommy, would be in all-day Pre-K.

This full-time opportunity never happened. The school district went above and beyond to keep my job for me for two years, but I ended up not going back for reasons I will include later in this memoir. I miss teaching every day. I gave no credit to myself back then, but now, in retrospect, feel justified in stating that I was a dedicated and talented teacher. I taught Spanish with an emphasis on conversation. I worked with my favorite books that made this happen so well and so easily, and my students loved how much they were able to speak. Every lesson was created to the best of my ability; I designed interesting, interactive, and very creative exercises for my students each day. I brought lots of energy and enthusiasm with me to every class. I kept students engaged in speaking, reading, and writing from bell to bell. Ninety minutes passed by in the "blink of an eye" for me and my students would often make comments about how fast the class went for them.

I tried to create a nonthreatening, comfortable, and encouraging working environment, where students felt accepted and safe and could thrive. I wanted my students to feel uninhibited and motivated to speak Spanish and to write it through nonstop creative activities. Ninety minutes was a great time frame to accomplish this.

I discovered this rule through my fifteen years of experience working with students: If students believe that their teacher works hard for them, they will, in turn, work hard for their teacher. If you engage them during the entire period with their best interests in mind, discipline problems rarely occur. My students and I had a great relationship—one of mutual appreciation and respect. That is, we did until November 23, 2001.

I still mourn the loss of that job every day. But God is good, and he keeps me in my place. I have had countless dreams that I am back in the classroom again; only this time, I make a mess in every way possible! I begin every morning searching for my classroom. I never remember the room number and wander the halls looking for a classroom without a teacher. I am unable to find any of my classrooms, and every class of mine is in a different room. My extreme incompetence embarrasses me causing me to go home and hide in shame. On the rare occasions when I do find my room, I fail to take attendance. I never have an accurate absentee record or grades for my quarterly report cards. I am disorganized and terribly incapable. I forget to grade tests or even give assignments to be graded. At the end of each quarter, to try and save myself, I make up a grade for each student, but I have no evidence recorded to justify these grades.

I was always so happy to wake up and discover that I was dreaming. What a relief to know that I am not committed to a job that I cannot handle. I think that, if these dreams were not so humiliating, I might have been tempted to go back to teaching.

I entered Kessler on December 16 and ended up going home on April 16. At Kessler I got to try many different wheelchairs. I was so excited to learn that there was a wheelchair on the market that allowed the user to stand up with the push of a button! This was a huge ego builder for me, because the more productive I am, the happier I am. A standing chair allowed me to stand up and wash dishes, clean countertops, cook, and go grocery shopping independently because I could still stand and make everything happen just like I had done before my injury.

In order to become independent, I had to learn how to drive again. When you have three young children—ages three, six, and seven—cooking and driving are not optional activities. I began driving lessons as soon as possible. Our car insurance covered the cost of a new van that would require a built-in ramp and all the modifications needed for me to drive. Once I received my ramp van,

I had to get my license reinstated with the modifications. I started driving lessons with Kessler's Driver Rehabilitation Program.

Despite my many accomplishments, as well as counting my blessings while taking each day one at a time, I started to spiral into a painful depression. When I was home, I was used to being a superwoman—one who conquered many accomplishments in a day and even in a month. My new reality hit me hard. How could I feel "super" again when I could not answer the doorbell or house phone quickly enough? We had no accessible laundry room yet, and I was unable to help with the laundry. I did not drive yet, which meant I could not go grocery shopping back then (supermarkets did not yet deliver in 2002). My "greatness" of old had to be redefined. The song in my heart had vanished and I so desperately wanted it back.

This brings me to the next miracle and what a divine intervention can do for the spirit. June 1, 2002 was a warm sunny Saturday. Tom's sister called me. She lived in a beautiful suburban area with a beautifully landscaped backyard with an inviting back deck for entertaining. Aunt Rosie called for permission to take the kids on Sunday. After all, she had a great outdoor pool, and my kids were all good swimmers. She had two young boys whose ages paired perfectly with my children. I eagerly accepted, grateful for her thoughtful invitation. I was not driving yet, so entertaining my children seven days a week was harder than ever. My three loved their cousins and would jump at any opportunity to see them. My depression seemed to be getting worse, and I could not seem to shake the feelings of extreme sadness. I was grieving my former, spectacular self—the self that felt invincible and completely in control, the self that used to be care free, pain free and fancy free.

Later that evening, after putting the kids to bed, I felt so sick of feeling sad. I gazed at the microwave and saw that it was 9:00 p.m. on the *dot*. I felt that hopeless downward spiral begin to unravel again. The night was still young; I would be up for at least another three hours, and my heart was shattered, broken; the despair was profoundly painful. I wanted the pain and anguish of the day to disappear, vanish, evaporate. I wanted it to go away now. I was too distraught to pray. I had not been to church in a few weeks, and all I said to God was, "Lord, you gotta do something to show me you care, because I don't even feel you in my life right now."

Tom and I decided to go to church on Sunday. We attended the 10:30 Mass as usual with our three children. Today was the celebration of Corpus Christi (the body of Christ), which for Catholics is, in the Eucharist, broken and shared every Sunday. Our pastor, Father Doug, celebrated every Mass that Sunday. There were five of them, beginning as early as 7:30 a.m. and continuing until the last Mass at 5:30 p.m. Usually, other priests shared the schedule to alleviate Father Doug's workload, but this particular Sunday, the five Masses all belonged to our dedicated pastor.

That beautiful Sunday morning in June, he started his homily by saying, "I began writing this homily at 9:00 last night. I finished at 2:30 in the morning, and it is a pretty good homily, if I do say so myself."

After the laughter of the congregation diminished, Father started his homily. I felt deeply loved and knew that my life would never be the same again—in a spiritual way. Father Doug's entire homily was about me and my entire family! Our holy pastor, who had devoted most of his life to serving and honoring the Lord, spoke highly of my family. He gave specific examples of things we had done or said in the past that had increased *his* faith as a priest and inspired him deeply.

He talked about my oldest son, Steven, and the reaction he had when he received the Eucharist for the very first time during his First Holy Communion. Father Doug explained that, after Mass, "Steven found me and told me how great he felt accepting Jesus as his personal Lord and Savior. He told me he felt so touched and wanted to know how I must feel as a priest when I take the host every week."

Father Doug gave other accounts of things that we as a family had done in the past and advice I had given him that had touched his life and had caused him to marvel at our faith.

Father Doug's homily was a life enhancer for me. From that Sunday forward, I knew my broken heart was in the palm of Jesus's hand, and I knew I would be okay. I just needed time to grieve and accept my new and "unimproved" broken self. The certain divine affirmation for me was that my greatest grief the night before was at exactly 9:00 p.m. according to the clock on my microwave. Father Doug stated that he had begun writing his "pretty good" homily exactly when I had begged God to do something to show me that he cared about me because I could not feel him in my life! Just then, I needed him the most, but I could not find him. I never thought I would get such an affirmative, undeniable, unmistakable answer so *quickly*.

The day's reinforcement of God's love and compassion did not stop with Mass's end—it only got better. There was a seminar offered after the 12:00 Mass. The seminar was "Linking Your Spiritual Well-Being with your Physical Health"—just the message I needed to hear. My strategic planner, (God) inspired Rosie, my sister-in-law, to want to care for my kids for the day so I could attend this conference.

When I wheeled into the meeting room, everybody seemed to know who I was; I felt like a celebrity. Parishioners hugged me and gave me some trinket gifts—one was a homemade crocheted cross that was a magnet for the Frigidaire. This insightful parishioner told me to put it on my refrigerator and, every time my eyes met it, to just say, "Thank God."

During the entire symposium, I felt wrapped in a hug. People were so nice, loving, and sympathetic, and they were singing my praises. Toward the end of this event, there was a table raffle. Everyone had signed his or her name at the beginning of the seminar because, by the afternoon's end, a raffle would be drawn from each table, and the winner from each would win their table's centerpiece. Each centerpiece was unique, but each one was a gorgeous sampling of plants with vibrant flowers in bloom that you could transplant directly into your garden or, perhaps, an even bigger pot to adorn a deck or front entrance of your home.

I knew that there was no possibility of me winning the raffle because I had never signed in. I could not write that well yet, and I did not want to exert the effort, so I decided to forfeit the opportunity. When the name was chosen from my table, the woman next to me was the one randomly chosen winner of the floral centerpiece.

The parishioner announced, "I am allergic to flowers, I give the basket to Jeanine Valenti."

I could not believe it! I had no chance of winning that centerpiece, and yet I did anyway. There is no limit to God's love and there is no way to separate ourselves from God's love once we acknowledge him as our Lord and Savior. And why would we want to?

This excerpt from the letter of Paul to the Romans (Romans 8:31–39, NLT) represents the reason why God created this special day for me as a direct and immediate answer to my prayer "God you gotta do something to show me you care, because I cannot feel you in my life right now…"

What shall we say about such wonderful things as these? If God is for us, who can ever be against us? Since he did not spare even his own son but gave him up for us all, won't he also give us everything else? Who dares accuse us who God has chosen for his own? No one— for God himself has given us *right* standing with himself. If God is for us, who then will condemn us? No one; for Christ Jesus died for us and was raised to life for us, and he is sitting in the place of honor at God's right hand, pleading for us.

Can anything ever separate us from Christ's love? Does it mean he no longer loves us if we have trouble or calamity or are persecuted or hungry or destitute or in danger or threatened with death? As the scriptures say, "For your sake we are killed every day; we are being slaughtered like sheep." No, despite all these things, overwhelming victory is ours through Christ, who loved us.

And I am convinced that nothing can separate us from God's love—neither death nor life, neither angels nor demons, and not our fears for today. No power in the sky above or on the earth below, indeed nothing in all creation, will ever separate us from the love of God that is revealed in Jesus Christ Our Lord.

In my experience, there are three primary reasons preventing people from accepting Jesus as their personal Lord and Savior:

- The whole story is "too far-fetched" to believe (the virgin birth, Jesus being raised from the dead).

- To believe in Jesus is blasphemy. There is only one God.
- Pride/stubbornness.

Let's look at the first objection. Atheists and agnostics have explained this view many times to me over the years. I always follow up with the question, "If God or a Master Creator does not exist, how did *we* get here?" I get one of two responses—by luck or by science. The first response is even more far-fetched than believing the biblical history before us. We are not single celled amoebas—we are very complex, intricately made, ingeniously constructed, and capable of great achievements. In my opinion, the best thing you can do for yourself and your families is to develop a relationship with God. Ask him to reveal himself to you. Keep a notepad with you and an open mind. With eyes wide open, prepare to be amazed.

Science explains the creation of the world as starting with the big bang theory—a colossal explosion that created the universe. I follow that with the question, "Who created the explosion?" No one has yet to give me any explanation other than, "It just happened," or, "It happened by chance." I am not science minded, so I will not expand on the science any further except to say that scientific experts agree that science and religion can coexist without contradiction.

Let's move on to objection number two, there is only *one* God. Therefore, the conclusion becomes that the belief that Jesus is a God or Messiah is blasphemous. Judaism and Islam have great respect for Jesus as a "messenger" of/for God. Muslims do believe in the miracle of a virgin birth, but neither religion believes that Jesus is the Messiah or "Savior" of the world. Christians believe in *the Trinity*, which some say is a mystery that is very hard to understand. I see this concept very clearly as the way it was explained by one of our priests, from St. Matthias. Father explained in his homily: Think of the sun. The sun cannot exist as "the sun" without three components—the *sun* (God), the *heat* the sun gives off (Jesus), and the *rays* of the sun (the Holy Spirit and the part of Jesus that is *always* available to and for us). Even in the middle of a rainy day, when the sun is nowhere in sight, one can take a plane and rise above the clouds where the sun is always shining somewhere. The sun is forever present to sustain us. You just need to know where to go and find it. Well, once we accept and invite Jesus into our hearts, he is *always* with us. And I feel that. All day, every day, I am walking with him. I want this for *everybody*—including people I do not know and never will.

As for objection number three, let's explore how destructive pride can be. Humor me for a minute. Think about a typical insect, such as the ant. Do you know that according to Google, ants can carry between ten and fifty times their body weight? Did you know that they spend their entire lives working? They only sleep for eight minutes every twelve hours. I have a lot of respect for ants. Imagine their lives for a painful moment. Because their brains are so small, they could never believe how easily we can find food. They could never comprehend that we have supermarkets where food is in one place and so easily attainable. They are *not capable* of understanding our world.

Well, we are like ants in comparison to God. True, God did create us in his image (Genesis 1:27), but that is a physical likeness. He is so high above us, incomprehensibly smarter than we could ever be. His heart is unfathomably bigger than ours, so he loves us more than we could ever love him, which excites me—because I love God with all my being (my body, mind, and soul.) This is why I *rarely* have a bad day even though three-quarters of my body is *paralyzed* and I am in constant pain!

What could an intimate relationship with God do for you? The Bible talks about the importance of being *humble*. Humility is a God-loving trait. Humility trumps stubborn pride. Pride can damage our soul because it limits our potential and often acts as an obstacle or barrier preventing a relationship that God desires for us.

I have separated a few Bibles passages that speak to this point:

- "As the heavens are higher than the earth, so are my ways higher than your ways and my thoughts than your thoughts" (Isaiah 55:9 NIV).

- "When pride comes, then comes disgrace, but with humility comes wisdom" (Proverbs 11:2, ESV).
- "Therefore, as God's chosen people, holy and dearly loved, clothe yourselves with compassion, kindness, humility, gentleness and patience" (Colossians 3:12, NIV).
- "In the same way, you who are younger submit yourselves to your elders. All of you, clothe yourselves with humility toward one another, because, "God opposes the proud but shows favor to the humble" (1 Peter 5:5, NIV).

There are many more scriptures favoring humility and condemning stubborn pride. I have just chosen a few of my favorites.

The ultimate sign of humility was shown right before Jesus died. He looked at the people who were mocking him and cheering his impending death and raised his eyes toward the sky and said, "Father, forgive them; for they know not what they do" (Luke 23:34, KJV).

So, my dear readers, do not kid yourselves by dismissing God or any of his requirements based on *your* logic. As much as the typical ant pales in comparison to ourselves as humans, so do our human ways and intelligence pale in comparison to God's. Do not lean on your own understanding, which can and, at some time, will fail you but, rather, educate yourself by understanding God's word and that his word will never fail you. He loves us and wants the very best outcome for you!

One of my co-workers asked me if I knew what B.I.B.L.E. stands for. I said, "No."

And he declared, "Basic Instructions Before Life's End."

"How true and clever!" I exclaimed.

Then I asked Google to come up with other solutions for the acronym. And it did not disappoint, returning Best Investment Before Life's End, Best Instruction Book for Living Eternally, and Best Instruction Book for Living Every day.

Chapter 8

To Church or Not to Church

I have heard dozens upon dozens of people say that one does not need a church to worship God. Logically, I agree. Practically speaking, I disagree.

Don't most of us agree that time flies by us? Many friends, for instance, may have sincere desires to "get together." But if a date is not secured right at the beginning of that desire, a week will turn into a month in what seems like "a blink of an eye." Or perhaps we have a book that has first priority on our reading list, but we can't seem to find the time. The insanity of life most often prevents us from dedicating ample time to accomplish what is important or even enjoyable to us. We also tend to take "tomorrow" for granted. We expect tomorrow to come. But the truth is, for many people, tomorrow does not come. This is why having life insurance is so important! We need to protect the ones we love, should the "tomorrow" we hope for not come. Think about yourself for a minute. What is *your* insurance policy should tomorrow not come?

I used to think you couldn't take anything with you when you die. I have come to realize that there is one great thing you can leave this world with, and that is a wonderful, warm, personal relationship with God, which, for Christians, also includes Jesus the Son and the Holy Spirit. Death is conquered. Your last breath on earth is your first breath in paradise, where life is blissful and eternal, *just as originally planned in the Garden of Eden, or the failed "Plan A"*!

Attending church on a regular basis makes it easier to make God a priority in your life so that the insanity of life does not get the best of you. One church, however, does not fit all. I recommend that you "trial" individual churches and see which ones best fit into your version of life. Every church has its own style. Which church will motivate you to be the *best Christian you can be*? Is it the one with different music styles because you love to sing and it makes you want to join the choir? Is it the church that does not have a choir but spends more time on its readings and homilies/sermons? Is it the church with the great Bible studies? Maybe the church you will like has a phenomenal prayer group, and you want to develop a skillful and meaningful prayer life. Maybe it will be the warm feeling you get when you walk through the doors. Finding the church that is right for you requires effort, but that effort will pay off!

As we are advised in an excerpt from The Letter from St. Paul to the Philippians 4:6–7 (NIV), "Do not be anxious about anything, but in every situation, by prayer and petition, with thanksgiving, present your requests to God, and the peace of God, which transcends all understanding, will guard your hearts and your minds in Christ Jesus."

If we can find a church that we can grow to love and attend regularly, we will grow in our faith, which is what Jesus desires for us. By getting spiritual nourishment through hearing scripture and receiving the Eucharist (body and blood of Christ), our hearts (where the Holy Spirit dwells) will start to gain strength. Since our heart is a muscle, joy naturally starts to increase in your life. It works for me. Don't rule out that it can work for you, too. God wants the same result for you as he has given to me. I just followed his recipe for success.

We can have the best of intentions, believing that the "tomorrow" will come. It will be *tomorrow* when you will activate your faith by regularly following that prayer book your grandmother gifted you at your confirmation ceremony in eighth grade. *Tomorrow*, you will dust off that Bible that has been on a shelf in your house for over a decade and finally start reading it. In the meantime, until your tomorrow arrives, your spirits are beginning to weaken because they are not getting the proper nourishment they need to stay strong and thrive in a world that needs God more than *ever*!

Lack of spiritual food can be as dramatic as atrophy, or dead muscles around the part of our hearts that Jesus has occupied since our baptism. During my Catholic baptism, my parents took vows to reject Satan and committed themselves before God to raise me as a follower of Jesus Christ. The Holy Spirit is the power of Christ that is able to enter and dwell within you as you try to navigate this world, full of evil, spiritually working against us because the "prince of this world" is also known as the "enemy" of this world, whose purpose is to steer you in the wrong direction. That "wrong" direction is against what God wants for us, and this "enemy" is great at deceiving us. More spiritual proof to reinforce this truth will come later in my memoir.

If you never were baptized, any Christian church will baptize you, but you will need another Christian to sponsor you. If you wish to be baptized into the Catholic faith, your sponsor must also be an active Catholic. By "active" you must be a participating member of a Catholic church.

If you have already been baptized but have been inactive in your faith, you need to invite him (he will come as three in one) to be more present in your life. I wholeheartedly recommend that you investigate a few Christian churches in your area to see which ones inspire you to reactivate your faith. Again, this will be an effort on your part, but the consequences will be priceless!

I am writing this memoir so that my future family might come to know me through this book. I am giving you the best advice I know. Technology advances so quickly. Right now, I just "ask Alexa" to play me a song, and she does. By the time you are reading this book, I can't even *imagine* how you might be getting your music! It can't be simpler than it is today, can it? Well, I recommend that you look up a song called "In This Place" by Trevor and Victoria Thompson

When I listen to this song, my heart overflows with love, gratitude, and admiration for a God, who loves us more than our human mind and heart can measure. I wish the same reaction for you.

IN THIS PLACE
by Trevor and Victoria Thompson

We are all hungry people
We need shelter and strength
We are one in our hurting
We are one in our pain

In our suffering and sadness
We are saved by the grace
Of the power and the spirit
That is here in this place

Chorus:

**We are gathered at the table
As one in the Lord
We are gathered as people
Who are living the word**

**Our hearts and our spirits
Are nurtured by grace
It is Jesus who fills us
He is here in this place**

All our lives are a mystery
We seek not where they lead
We are asked now to trust you
And we know we must believe

As our feet become Christ's feet
We go forth with grace
Of the power and the spirit
That is here in this place

Chorus

Though the world may tell us
To look at ourselves
We reach to one another
Where suffering dwells

As our hands become Christ's hands
We are healed by the grace
Of the power and the spirit
That is here in this place

Chorus

In the bread that is broken
Is the Christ that restores
As we take now receive Him
We find love evermore

As the bread becomes body
We are filled with the grace
Of the power and the spirit
That is here in this place

Chorus

Chapter 9

Why Bad Things Happen to Good People

We would not be human if we didn't wonder, why do bad things happen to good people? In our humanness, we want to know—it bothers us that life is not fair. It goes against human logic when we see bad or tragic things happen to seemingly innocent people. Through conversations with many throughout my lifetime, I have heard people pondering, "Why me?" or, "Why her?" Often, they conclude with, "Everything happens for a reason," or, "God only gives you what you can handle."

I have plenty to say about each of these answers. I am confident that I got my question answered by God directly. Why do bad things happen to good people? In my heart, I knew that it was not God's will. That makes no sense when God is love and we are his children. My answer was given to me while I was asleep, and it jolted me awake; it was the perfect response, which I respectfully honor today as divinely answered by God himself.

I never believed for a second that God caused my injury. That did not stop me from being angry at my outcome and disappointed that God had not prevented my injury from happening. My children and I, as young as I can remember, would say our prayers every night. We would thank God for something different that happened that day. But the very last sentence of a varied prayer was always, "And keep us safe from harm."

We never said, "And please don't *cause* us harm," because his harming us was not a possibility. Would a father purposely cause harm or pain to his child? It happens, but rarely, because it is not natural and goes *against* parental instincts, nature, and reason.

I did think that God could *protect us from* tragedy, and asking him to do that, to me, was a reasonable request. My children and I asked God to protect us from harm and keep us safe every night in our prayers.

During the early days of my injury, I was angry and disappointed that I had not been protected from my present fate. I felt betrayed and angry. Then I remembered that, during January 2001, my car had been stolen out of our garage and then found by police ten days later in a warehouse in Newark, New Jersey, where it was being stripped for parts. It was nearly totaled with damages, but my insurance company restored it to its original state, and I was still driving it. Perhaps God was trying to protect me from an ill-fated future by allowing it to get stolen from my garage?

When that attempt failed, I thought of something else that enlightened me. Twenty days before my accident, Tom and I took the kids to Florida's Disney World. We rented a standard run-of-the-mill car. It was early November after the tragedy of 9/11. People were afraid to fly and were very intimidated by terrorism. As a result, thousands of flights were canceled. The car rental upgraded us to a Mitsubishi Montero, which was an SUV. I loved the way it drove, which made me hate my current vehicle even more than I already did. I vowed that, when I got home, I would trade in my old SUV for a Montero. That was my plan.

I got home on November 10 but did not execute this plan in time to change my fate. To this day, I believe that the good Lord was still trying to separate me from my irresponsibly-engineered SUV and negate my ill-fated destiny.

I then went over the events of that day. It was a Friday, and my colleague had just lost her mom after a long fight with breast cancer. The wake was from 2:00 p.m. to 4:00 p.m. and 7:00 p.m. to 9:00 p.m. I planned on leaving my house at 2:30 to get there by 2:45 and would stay an hour and come home in time to be at my friend's house for dinner. Her two boys were the same ages as my boys, and I was excited to have the night off from cooking and connect with dear friends.

Then I got a phone call from another colleague asking me if I was attending the wake. When I told her I was, she told me that we (the World Language Department) planned to meet as a group at 2:30 p.m. I said I was unaware of that plan, but I would adjust my schedule accordingly. That phone call altered my time line and changed my fate.

As I was getting ready to leave, my daughter hugged my leg, begging me not to go. "Mommy, Mommy! Please don't go. Stay here with me."

I replied that I would not be gone long, and when I returned, we would go to a friend's house for dinner.

As soon as I got in my car, my husband called me over to our second driveway to his car. "Come here, hon. I have something to show you."

I sighed. Another holdup. *I just want to leave for the wake so I can meet with my group on time!* I thought to myself. I got out of the car and half-heartedly viewed the purchases Tom had made earlier that morning. He had bought the shelving for our new walk-in closet, as well as new carpeting, and he was very proud of his selections. I agreed that they were all very nice.

I was feeling so great and on top of the world because of the hour-long aerobic workout I had just taken, and I wanted to wrap my arms around him and give him a wonderful, slow, and affectionate kiss. I thought about it, but I did not take the time to do so. I had tunnel vision. I was a woman on a mission to get to a wake.

As you can imagine, I am still disappointed after twenty years of being injured that I did not take the more sensual route. Leaving one minute later would have changed my fate. You know the saying—hindsight is twenty-twenty.

But I chose to get in my car without the kiss, kept my gratitude to Tom to myself, and went on my "merry way." Only my "way" was not "merry" at all. I left my driveway at 2:07, and by 2:09, my car had flipped upside down, and my C6-C7 vertebrae was broken and my spinal cord was crushed. I found out soon enough that an unwanted side effect of a broken neck is also a broken heart.

To this day, I credit God for Marisa's reaction in trying to delay or cancel my departure. I also credit God for inspiring Tom to call me over to further delay my exit, as well as making me thirsty for a kiss I deprived myself of receiving. My question to God is, "Lord, you know how headstrong I am. Why couldn't you have given me a flat tire? That would have worked!"

I have not yet received an answer. He may have tried. Perhaps he put some upside-down nails in my pathway. but I may have failed to "hit the nail on the head" the right way to get a flat!

To the people who say, "Everything happens for a reason," I agree with you. God gives us free will. In the United States, as Americans, we live freely. I am paralyzed because I was seated in an unsafe SUV. The accident happened, not because God made it happen but, rather, because the other driver did not go home to sleep after his all-night shift. He got off work in the morning and went to work at another job without resting first. I was the consequence of a bad decision. On the way home, he fell asleep two miles before his final destination.

Free will has consequences—some good, some not so good, some indifferent, and some tragic. God gives us the free will to love him or leave him. God rewards those who choose to love him greatly and richly. What meaning would love have to him if we were automatically engineered to do so?

Now, for the final and most meaningful answer to the original question, why do bad things happen to good people?

There is good in our world and evil in our world. For some reason, right now, the Prince of Darkness is in control of our world. God can take it back under his control but presently chooses not to. That is the mystery. But I have scriptural proof that Satan's time to influence the world is now.

We are told in The Letter from St. Paul to the Ephesians 6:12 (KJV), "For we wrestle not against flesh and blood, but against principalities, against powers, against the rulers of the darkness of this world, against spiritual wickedness in high places."

Paul wrote this to the people of Ephesus, who struggled with similar problems that still exist today and Paul explains to his new Christian population that our enemies are not human but, rather, spiritual. We struggle against the evil network of this world.

The "prince of this world" is mentioned well over two hundred times in the Bible. A passage in the Second Letter from St. Paul to the Corinthians, 4:4 (ASV), states, "The God of this world has blinded the minds of the unbelieving so that they might not see the light of the gospel as the glory of Christ, who is the image of God." Paul is the author of this letter to the people of Corinth after he traveled there to explain this new Christian faith after Jesus rose from the dead, proving that what our Savior had proclaimed all along had come to pass.

Jesus alone went off to pray and fast in the desert. He was there for forty days and forty nights. Toward the end of his time there, Satan took Jesus up to the highest mountain with a beautiful and vast view as far and wide as the eye can see.

In Matthew 4:8–11 (NLT), "Satan took Jesus to the peak of a very high mountain and showed him the nations of the world and all their glory. 'I will give it all to you,' Satan said, 'if you will only kneel and worship me.' Jesus replies, 'Get out of here, Satan, the scriptures say, Worship only the Lord God, Obey only Him!'"

This scripture tells us that the world is Satan's to give. Otherwise, Jesus would have denied that the world was Satan's to give and would have called him a *liar* or *deceitful*. But Jesus did not because, in this situation, he knew the world did and still does belong to Satan, and right now is Satan's time.

When the time is right (and only God knows when that will be), Jesus will come again. He will return to the earth and make it his. There are scriptures that verify this, Revelation 1:7, Matthew 24, and Revelation 19:11–16 to name just a few.

Now for the moment I have been waiting to be revealed. It is human nature to ask, "why me?" when things don't go right. I gave myself permission to *shout* this question. "Lord, why me? Haven't I had enough tragedy in my life?" My brother Lenny was taken from us when he was only three and half years old, breaking my parents' hearts. I had a handicapped twin, and then Mom died young. And more heartbreak has happened; my brothers were both alcoholics who barely functioned, and one died prematurely at fifty-nine. "I am now the last sibling in my family to meet tragedy! How much can one family take? Why, Lord, why? Tell me why!"

That same night that I called out to God in despair, I was awakened from a *dead* sleep with the answer to the same question I had posed to God. And the answer makes so much sense—especially since Satan's time is now. The divine answer I received was this: When a faithful follower and lover of God goes through life happily, and lives a life that is pleasing to God, Satan might set out to hurt that child of God with the hope of having three layers of beautiful satisfaction by hurting a believer:

- Satan wants to hurt a child of God because he wants the victim to blame God and become mad at God. And the best hope of all? The victim's faith in God might weaken or, better yet, be destroyed.
- Satan hopes to purposely and intentionally hurt God.
- The enemy also hopes to shatter the faith among the victim's friends and family. Satan wants the faith-filled to blame God for their problems so they might lose their godly faith. That is Satan's main goal for everyone and he uses his network of evil to harm as many believers as possible.

Satan doesn't need to touch the faith of a nonbeliever or a person who is already miserable with drug addiction, suffering from depression, or in a terrible place in life. This person is already where the network of evil wants him—depressed and downtrodden. Satan and his huge network of evil lovers will try to hurt someone who has a lot to lose, such as happiness and faithfulness. He wants to take as many people down with him as he can.

Once that message was made known to me, I never questioned life's most despicable events, such as the Holocaust, gruesome murders, the abuse of children, infants found in dumpsters, violence, drug addiction, and disease. Satan's network of evil is all around us (for now) and its mission is to weaken, kill, and destroy your faith in God and your love for God, along with your admiration and respect for all that is divine.

You have heard the saying, "Misery loves company." The prince of this world wants to rob you of your faith and cause you to question God's existence.

In Matthew 7:13–14 (NIV), Jesus warns his followers, "Enter through the narrow gate. For wide is the gate and broad is the road that leads to destruction, and many enter through it. But small is the gate and narrow the road that leads to life and only a few find it."

And in Luke 13:23–25 (NIV), someone asked Jesus:

"Lord, are only a few people going to be saved?"

He said to them, "Make every effort to enter through the narrow door because many, I tell you that many of you will try to enter, but will not be able. When once the owner of the house gets up and shuts the door, you will stand outside knocking and pleading, 'Sir, open the door to us.' But he will answer, 'I do not know you or where you come from.'"

This reading goes on to say that the people outside of the door will begin to wail, and there will be desperation and gnashing of teeth. To merely go to church is not enough to be saved. One must sincerely love God, because, if you do, you will *want* to live the life he recommends, which is to understand his teachings and follow them. This will take more effort on your part, but it is well worth it because it will lead you toward that narrow path few find.

One more final thought as we end this chapter. If this is the devil's time right now, then James 4:4 (NIV) makes perfect sense. "You adulterous people! Don't you know that friendship with the world means enmity against God? Therefore, anyone who chooses to be a friend of the world becomes an enemy of God."

While you are here, enjoying the life God gave you, you can be permanently saved. You are guaranteed to find that narrow path very easily if you accept Jesus into your life as your personal savior from damnation. And when this happens and Jesus becomes the occupier of your heart, you will be attracted to his words like magnets are attracted and secured to steel. Your place in heaven will be secured, and your soul will be transformed. With this transformation comes a great exhilarating feeling that, once you get to know it, you will never want to be separated from it.

My beloved parents, Jeanne Magill Rankin + Eugene Julius Senerote got married on April 24, 1948

Frances Rankin holding Jeanine (left) and Jeanne R. Senerote holding Francine (right) 2/65

Sunday after church, 1965—Jeanine (left), Francine (right)

Flatbush Ave., Brooklyn 2007…My memories of small businesses within walking distance to home.

Our family's place of worship. Holy Cross Church,
Brooklyn New York 1945-1972

P.S. 181- I remember walking to school here like it was yesterday, 1969-
1971. 1971-1972 was transferred to the "mini-school" down the street.

Easter Sunday, 1969
Francine (left) and Jeanine (right)

Tom and Jeanine united as one on July 20ᵗʰ, 1991

Thanksgiving Day, November 22, 2001—Day before my accident

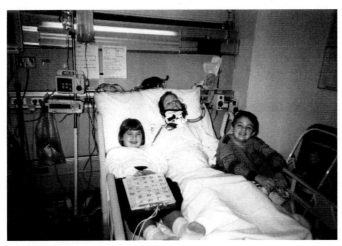

December, 2001 post-spinal fusion surgery, ICU, Robert Wood Johnson Hospital. Marisa holding a letter chart so I could communicate without the audibility of voicing the slightest whisper.

My beautiful and beloved Colombian family. We reunited in 2017 after 37 years apart in Medellin, Colombia. From left: Blanca Lucia, Maria Adelaida, me (rising to the occasion), Ana Lucia, Maria Teresa, Back row, Walther + wife Catalina

Meeting Maria Adelaida after 37 years! In 2017, brought my original photos taken in 1982, located on the front table.

Tommy (nine years old), Eddie (seven years old)
Lenny (three years old). Photo taken in 1957

Welcome to the world, Santino, our first miracle
baby. Photo taken in January, 2020.

Mike, Brittany, Santino (three years old) and Stella, (one year old)

Chapter 10

The Miracles of Jesus

A summarized account of just some of the many miracles Jesus performed:

- **John 21:25 (NIV)**. Jesus did many other things as well. If every one of them were written down, I suppose that even the whole world would not have room for the books that would be written.
- **John 2:1–11**. Jesus turned water into wine at a wedding when the supply of wine ran out.
- **John 4:46–47**. Jesus cured the nobleman's son.
- **Luke 5:1–11**. Jesus enables a great haul of fishes.
- **Mark 1:30–31**. Jesus cured Peter's mother-in-law of a fever.
- **Mark 1:40–45**. Jesus healed a leper.
- **Matthew 8:5–13**. Jesus healed the centurion's servant.
- **Luke 7:11–18**. Jesus raised the widow's son from the dead.
- **Matthew 8:23–27**. Jesus stilled the storm.
- **Matthew 8:28–34**. Jesus healed two demoniacs.
- **Matthew 9:1–8**. Jesus cured the paralytic.
- **Matthew 9:18–26**. Jesus raised a ruler's daughter from the dead.
- **Luke 8:43-48**. Jesus cured a woman of the issue of blood.
- **Matthew 9:27–31**. Jesus opened the eyes of two blind men.

- **Matthew 9:32–33.** Jesus loosened the tongue of a man who could not speak.
- **John 5:1–9.** Jesus healed an invalid man at the pool called Bethesda.
- **Matthew 12:10–13.** Jesus restored a withered hand.
- **Matthew 12:22.** Jesus cured a demon-possessed man
- **Matthew 14:15–21.** Jesus begins feeding a crowd with 2 fish
- **Matthew 15:34–39.** Jesus fed at least five thousand people with five loaves of bread and two fish.
- **Matthew 15:22–28.** Jesus healed a woman of Canaan.
- **Mark 7:31–37.** Jesus cured a deaf and mute man.
- **Mark 8:22–26.** Jesus opened the eyes of a blind man.
- **Matthew 17:14–21.** Jesus cured a boy who was plagued by a demon.
- **John 9:1-38.** Jesus opened the eyes of a man born blind.
- **Luke 13:10–17.** Jesus cured a woman afflicted eighteen years.
- **Luke 14:1–4.** Jesus cured a man of leprosy.
- **Luke 17:11–19.** Jesus cleansed and cured 10 lepers.
- **John 11:1–46.** Jesus raised Lazarus from the dead.
- **Matthew 20:3–34.** Jesus opened the eyes of two blind men.
- **Matthew 21:18–22.** Jesus caused the fig tree to wither.
- **Luke 22:50–51.** Jesus restored the ear of a high priest's servant.
- **Luke 24:5–6.** Jesus rose from the dead.
- **John 21:1–14.** The second great haul of fishes.

Millions upon millions, equaling billions of people have been born into or have converted to Christianity over the centuries, but not because Jesus said that he is the Son of God. People did not bow down to Jesus because of what he *said*. People believe him for what he had *done*, which was to perform immeasurable miracles. *And the greatest of all miracles was rising from the dead*, although Jesus could not have performed that one. This one came from God, proving that this miracle was the Father's plan for the redemption of humankind whom he loves.

At Jesus's death, a very nasty thunderstorm erupted. The curtain in the Jewish temple, which separated the people from the most sacred altar available to only the highest chief priest, ripped in half lengthwise. This rendering of the curtain symbolized that no longer would there be separation between God and His people. Jesus could now dwell within the hearts of anyone who sought him by desiring a relationship with him.

I am convinced that, through my tragic accident, Satan and his evil network tried to break my faith, along with my spirit. I am so grateful that he did not; instead, the opposite happened. My faith got stronger. My love for God through Christ Jesus has transformed me. And I am convinced, as I wrote earlier, I am under the Good Lord's umbrella of protection.

I decided to celebrate this spiritual victory by hiring an artist to paint a small, soffit-sized mural on the archway from the dining room to the family room. It depicts a scriptural quote by God saying, in John 15:5 (KJV), "I am the vine and you are the branches; whoever abides by me and I in him, bears much fruit." A grape vine nourishes bunches of beautiful grapes all throughout the archway. This was my way of sending the evil network back to hell where it belongs. Their goal of weakening my faith and breaking my spirit has backfired in a most strong and profound way.

As years have passed, I realized that my extraordinary strength is not coming from me—it is flowing through me; and apart from the Father, the Son, and the Holy Spirit I can do nothing. All grace and strength are freely given through following God's son Jesus and allowing the blood he shed *for* me to work its way *through* me.

One of my favorite scriptures that I live out *every day* comes from Philippians, 4:13 (KJV) "I can do all things through Christ who strengthens me." It was at my weakest point in life when I realized how strong of a woman I am because of the protection he offers me, the spiritual encouragement he gives me, and the financial gifts he allows me.

All of these gifts empower me to be confident, trusting, and courageous. When I stop and think of all the things that could happen to me, I could easily find myself too vulnerable and scared to venture out of my house into a cruel and unpredictable world. Instead, I trust blindly that he will guide my paths, which run parallel with safety. In twenty years, my God has not disappointed me or abandoned my needs in any way. And for that, I am most grateful and humble.

Above all, he wishes this for everyone, including you!

Notes

Notes

Chapter 11

My Journey Forward

When I reflect on my last twenty years of being injured, I am in awe of the human body, how blessed I am to have such a high quality of life, despite the many health risks that come with a SCI. Without the promise of eternal life and a faithful God who keeps his promises and without the love and respect of my family, I could not be this optimistic.

From the first conscious day after my neck surgery, I made a decision that I have clung to every day since. I decided to minimize the effects of my injury on the well-being and peace of mind for my family. From the first hour home, I received a chair that stood me up. From the first day home, because of the great love I have for my family, I have never lost my inspiration to excel and overachieve. As stated earlier, I did have a "spiraling down" of emotions as the reality of my condition settled in. But I quickly called the social worker I had met and worked with while an inpatient at Kessler and asked her if we could meet again.

To my benefit, she informed me that she lived in the next town over. When she finished up with her private patients, she literally passed right by my neighborhood and could stop by on her way home. She and I met every week for a year. After that, we decided I had adjusted just fine, and we no longer needed to meet regularly. But I was sad to see her go; we had really enjoyed our time together.

In the meantime, besides therapy sessions, I had gotten my new adaptive license through Kessler's driver's rehab program. I'd learned to drive a new modified minivan equipped with hand controls and a ramp that folds and unfolds with a push of a button, either on my key fob or in my van.

I was starting to feel very victorious, like I had climbed my own personal Mount Everest. I had started taking control of my life again. Now, if only I could control my bowels.

I had learned at Kessler what a neck injury was. The neck is considered part of the "cervical spine," and it has seven vertebrae, C1 through C7. The lower the number, the worse the injury. For example, if you break your C1, (the first neck bone under your brain stem), chances are you will die because the C1 controls your diaphragm. The muscles that control your diaphragm are instantly paralyzed, and the victim suffocates unless they get immediate medical attention. If a person survives the initial impact, he or she will be dependent upon a respirator to control breathing for the rest of his or her life.

If your injury is from C1 to C3 and C4, the arms are paralyzed as well, including the hands. I saw a lot of these injuries as an inpatient.

My injury is the lowest neck injury you can get. But it is the *highest* number of 7, C6/C7, falling under the umbrella term *quadriplegia* or *tetraplegia*—C6/C7. I have use of my arms, but my left hand has much more dexterity and function than my right. I was born right dominant, but my left hand had no trouble picking up the slack and taking over.

There is a bump that can be felt on the lower part of the neck in the back. That bump is your C7 vertebra. Any trauma occurring *lower* than C7 falls under the umbrella term *paraplegia*. A paraplegic experiences paralysis from the lumbar or thoracic spine down, which means that there may be a very slight weakness of the trunk muscles. But paraplegics have full use and strength of their arms and hands, with paralysis in the legs, for sure.

What do paraplegics and quadriplegics have in common? Well, both are wheelchair dependent because neither can walk. And both injuries result in trouble controlling the bowel and bladder. Both injury levels must watch for skin breakdown, as blood circulation problems cause skin to become thinner and more prone to bruising and developing what we think of as "bedsores."

My first day at Kessler, my nurses were delighted to inform Tom and me that I had beautiful, tough skin and that we would not have to worry about skin breakdown. We never figured out how they could tell so quickly. But twenty years post injury, and I have never suffered from a pressure sore. And I am so grateful.

A skin sore can happen within a few minutes, so I was taught the importance of doing "weight shifts." This is a practiced method of shifting the body weight from the butt to other less stressed parts of the body. This is executed by lifting your backside up off the wheelchair and locking your arms at your elbows, using your armrests. This was no problem for me. I had a standing chair and stood up many times a day, doing dishes, making coffee, cooking, cleaning. I never had to worry about shifting my weight.

I learned how to manage my bladder also. I remember that day well. I had *finally* learned how to transfer myself from the elevated exercise mat in the gym to my wheelchair! What a hard-earned victory. I felt inspired and motivated now to gain an extra step of independence.

I raced back to my room and looked for my nurse. I wanted to give her the good news myself. I felt like I had climbed to the top of Mount Everest. I approached one of my favorite nurses. "Hi, Nurse Donna! Guess what?"

Her eyes looked as bright and gleaming with expectation as one would expect from a child in a candy store. "What?" she asked me.

"I learned how to transfer from my wheelchair to the exercise mat and from the mat back into my wheelchair!" I said triumphantly.

"That's fantastic," Donna agreed.

"So, now," I said, "I can practice getting on and off the toilet, so I can lose my indwelling catheter and ankle bag and pee on my own!"

Donna's exuberant smile gently faded as she explained that I did not have control of the muscle that controls my bladder, so I would still need the help of a catheter and a leg bag. My hope in this area crashed to the floor, and I cried on and off for a *week* over this disappointment.

I read many research studies and learned that, because I had a bladder tube placement starting from my urethra and ending in my bladder, going forward, I would be very susceptible to bladder infections. I had to learn to recognize the symptoms and report signs of infection to the doctor.

To this day, twenty years later, my doctor believes me when I tell him I have a urinary tract infection. And he calls in an antibiotic for me at the pharmacy when my infection is bad enough to cause extreme fatigue, bladder spasms, and white crystals gathering in my catheter tube. When I must take a nap, while I lay horizontal, if my bladder spasms in protest of the pain, causing urine to leak from my bladder through my urethra and not my catheter, I know I need treatment. By the time my second subscribed antibiotic pill is ingested, symptoms quickly disappear. By the fifth or seventh day, I return to my pre-infectious self, which is always a welcomed relief.

I need to wait as long as possible before taking my prescribed antibiotic in order to minimize my chances of becoming immune to an antibiotic that effectively kills the usual bacteria that cause my infection. After the infection clears up, I usually experience renewed energy, and that is always gratefully accepted.

I also found out that, as I get older, my skin will become weaker, and my body's ability to fight infections will lessen. Statistically, my condition will eventually lower my life expectancy by approximately ten to fifteen years. I try to make every day count. For me personally, this is not by binge-watching a series of movies or shows but, rather, by doing something productive and meaningful for a beloved charity every day. This, for me, fuels my soul, mood, and positive attitude— which is contagious to others.

The more I learned about spinal cord injuries, the more reasons I found to cry. I learned what I needed to know but, thankfully, not all at once. That would have been too much. I lived the first two years of my injury one day at a time, learning of its disappointments one at a time, grieving the loss of each one. I was gentle with myself and tried to celebrate each accomplishment as it came.

A big achievement was driving. I felt victorious behind the steering wheel as I operated everything with my hands, which got strength from my arms. Soon, gratitude became my favorite feeling—especially when I came to realize how much more important your arms are than your legs.

My left hand started getting stronger. My five fingers were steadily gaining dexterity, and my right hand could close with a flick of my wrist. My fingers on my right hand could not move independently of one another but my right hand could hold light objects—including the all-too-important blow-dryer! This was a *hallelujah* moment for sure.

I was grateful when my wheelchair allowed me to stand while I used both hands to wash dishes and scrub pots. I was joyful when I drove myself to the grocery store and picked out my own groceries using a red or green courtesy basket. I was amazed at how many bags of groceries I could get from one courtesy basket! And, when one basket is not enough, I often ask the employees behind the courtesy desk to hold basket number one for me while I busy myself filling a second one. After my groceries are gathered and paid for, the cashiers help me place the shopping bags on both sides of my chair, enabling me to drive them securely on my chair; into my car; and, ultimately, into my house, where I can proudly stand up and load the refrigerator and pantry.

It gave me so much satisfaction to feel like I led a life as rich as an able-bodied person. The more productive I was, the higher my spirits became. The song was back in my heart, and God helped me get it there. For that, I am forever deeply grateful!

Chapter 12

That Was Then, This Is Now

I am only human and flawed. I follow human nature. I am of average intelligence. I was hit hard and had to accept my brokenness. Many people who are reading this have or are experiencing a broken heart because of a tragedy in their lives. Before acceptance can occur, several stages must be completed. A human newborn cannot physically walk. That would be genetically impossible. Trunk and leg muscles must be exercised and developed first, and there is a natural process to get them there. As the trunk muscles and arms develop, a baby learns to turn over, sit up, and crawl. Then come the next steps—standing; walking; and, eventually, running.

Before we can truly accept a tragedy, we must go through the process and emotional pain of experiencing a sequence of steps. For me, it was heart throbbing; and as much as I wanted to, I could not sidestep the pain. In order to get past the pain, I had to go right through it. And it was excruciating!

The five stages of grief begin with *denial*. I thought I would walk again. And when I didn't, the second stage brought me to *anger*. Anger causes exhaustion and is very unpleasant to experience because it can be all-consuming and overwhelming.

I found this to be self-destructive and unsettling. To deal with the intensity of it, I reached out to my pastor one Sunday after church. I cried through my explanation of all that I had lost, bladder and bowel control, independence. I cried about my dependence on

Tom for dressing or transferring into bed or to my shower chair. I cried about having to sit four hours every other day, just to have a bowel movement, only to get into bed and have a bowel accident in the middle of the night that Tom was forced to clean up. I was also mad that "God" had allowed this to happen. There, I had laid it all out—all at my pastor's feet. I was *mad!* And I felt *terrible!*

Father suggested that I write the drowsy driver a letter and include all of my emotions but that I not send it. I did just that; in it, my pain and anger are apparent:

Julio,

My name is Jeanine, allow me to introduce myself. I am the young woman you hit broadside on November 23, 2001, at 2:09 p.m. just before the Paulus Boulevard jughandle on Route 18 in New Brunswick.

You did not intend to fall asleep; nor did you set out to hurt me. When your car hit mine, you escaped without injury. My SUV flipped, the roof caved in, and my neck was broken at thirty-six years of age. You left this scene of the accident and went on with your life. I, on the other hand, had suffered a severe spinal cord injury and became a quadriplegic. I am confined to a wheelchair. My independence and mobility were taken from me in one cruel split second.

You went home that day to be with your family. I went to Robert Wood Johnson Hospital to undergo eight hours of emergency surgery and fight for my life! I remained in the ICU for three and a half weeks. During this time, I could not breathe on my own and was hooked up to a respirator. I could not eat, drink, or talk for a month. In fact, I could not even muster a whisper. At the time, my children were three, six, and seven years old.

I wish you could have been present to see the tears fall from their eyes when they visited me in the hospital when I had five machines hooked up to me, from November 23, 2001 through December 16, 2001. I remained in the ICU as my body fought to free itself from infection and high fevers while remaining strong enough to breathe without the aid of a respirator.

What were you doing during this time?

From December 16, 2001 through April 16, 2002, I was an inpatient at Kessler Institute for Rehabilitation in West Orange, where I exercised four *hours a day* for four months to get my strength back. I am paralyzed from the chest down and had to learn how to roll over *without* the help of my muscles. I had to spend *hours* learning how to dress myself. This thirty-second task before my injury now took two hours to do after four months of practice. My wonderful husband now dresses me every day in twenty minutes in order to spare me the two hours of this mandatory and energy-draining activity.

I was separated from my husband and beautiful children for five long months. This separation was the hardest of all. My heart physically ached and often throbbed to be reunited with my family. *Every day* since November 23, 2001, I have been struggling to reclaim my life. I am seeking closure—this is the final stage of my healing process. In order to do this, I need for *you* to understand what you have done.

You now know that I am confined to a wheelchair—but this is not enough for me to gain closure. I need you to understand that the physical part of seeing me in a wheelchair only represents 50 percent of my injury. It is important to me that you know that, at the time of our accident, I was teaching Spanish to public high school students and religion to young students through my church. In one unfair second, my students had no teacher, and my precious and innocent children had no mother by their side at home.

Secondly, because of the severity of my injury, my bladder does not work. I, therefore, must keep an indwelling catheter placed inside my urethra at all times, and my urine, with the help of gravity, is collected in a plastic leg bag, which is strapped to my ankle. I empty the bag as needed throughout my day into a toilet.

Thirdly, because of my spinal cord injury, my bowels don't work. This means that I cannot control them. Because of this, I take three types of medication, which help with the digestion process. Every other day, I sit in the bathroom and wait for nature to take its course.

This takes between two and three and a half hours! What are you doing every-other day from 9:00 p.m. to midnight?

Fourthly, because of the severity of my injury, my feet and ankles swell. This is due to a lack of circulation. Because of this medical weakness, my blood pressure is chronically low. It went from textbook perfect (120/70) to a very low 90/70. This means I am always tired and feel drained. I chronically will always lack energy and can fall asleep anywhere, especially when I am not talking and filling my brain with oxygen.

Lack of circulation also causes skin breakdown, which can lead to pressure sores and constant bed rest to aid the slow healing process. This condition can cause massive infection and, ultimately, an early death.

Finally, because of my spinal cord injury, my legs move uncontrollably without permission from my brain. I must take muscle relaxers to make these "spasms" bearable.

I am a Christian woman who stands firmly in faith. I rely on Jesus Christ and his partnership with God Almighty to carry me through my many everyday struggles. I am deeply grateful that, by the grace of God, I am not angry or bitter. I am heartbroken, but this is different than being angry or bitter. These two emotions can eat away at your soul and damage your spirit and well-being. I know that, in taking up my cross and following Jesus, I am required to forgive you.

I am finding it hard to forgive you when you have made no attempt to contact me with so much as an apology. I find this lack of concern on your part *unacceptable*. I think of you *every day*. I consider you a *coward* for not having the decency to apologize to me and acknowledge your wrongdoing and my daily struggles. For that, you should feel ashamed.

I hope this letter causes you to toss and turn in your bed for a night or two. And when you are tossing and turning, thank God, because I cannot toss or turn. When my position becomes uncomfortable, I must wake up my husband, who then has to get up from the bed and turn me to a new position!

Before I end this letter, I want to talk about the cost of this injury. One month of ICU care, neck fusion surgery, and four months of rehabilitation cost much more than a million dollars. Then there is the cost of the wheelchair, which was $47,000. My elevator to get me to my bedroom was $40,000, and my very specialized van, which is modified to enable me to drive it, was another $75,000. Then, I needed ramps installed, which allow me to come and go as I choose. These concrete and wooden ramps were about $25,000. I am telling you all of this to make you understand another deficiency on your part. The liability portion of your car insurance was terribly inadequate. It offered me $15,000. That amount did not even cover my emergency room expenses for the first day!

I also am required to pay $400 per month to have my house cleaned, because I cannot do it myself, along with not being able to do what I do best, which is teaching! This accident will also cost me my career and my ability to earn a salary and will cost me hundreds of thousands of dollars in expenses.

In a perfect world, you would be the one cleaning my house and doing my laundry or at least paying for it!

In conclusion, I have done my best and have worked my hardest to get my wonderful life back. You have done nothing to help, and that, along with an apology, was the least you should have done.

This letter was purposely never sent to my offender, but as I had hoped, would prove to be very therapeutic, and I was able to let go of my anger quickly. I am very grateful, because holding onto that anger was very painful and unpleasant, not to mention counterproductive! But it was essential that I experience it in order to heal properly. An important lesson in life is that you do not forgive for the benefit of the offender. The value in forgiveness is it sets the Forgiver free.

The next stage leading to acceptance is *bargaining*. This next step was not nearly as painful for me as was the anger. I mentioned this stage earlier in my book, when I told God all about "my" plan for "my" happy ending. I asked for God to restore my paralysis, and I, in turn, would speak of this miracle, in which good had conquered the evil and injustices of life. I would carry a "before" and "after"—a "then" and "now"—picture and would bring people to God every day.

I visited a nun who claimed she possessed the gift of healing. Tom and I took the seven-hour journey out past Bangor, Maine, to meet the sister, who would pray over me and demand that the devil leave me and that God enable me to "rise up" and "walk," When it did not happen, Sister told me it could happen within the next two days.

I also flew Sister out to my house to hold a healing mass for the parishioners of St. Matthias. I contacted each person on our parish sick list. Seventy-five people came and prayed for individual and group healing. Sister prayed with each attendant individually and personally. She pleaded that God restore and heal each person in attendance, including me.

I continued in this stage as I underwent years of Bible study and read dozens of spiritual books, trying to gain God's good favor and blessings.

The "next" stage of *depression* came and went, and I still considered myself to be *bargaining*. During the "depression" stage, I sought therapy and lots of support through lunching and munching with friends.

It was through my last stage of *acceptance* that I realized that the Lord had, *indeed, healed me*!

I was looking at being "healed" through one lens as walking on my own two feet. Now, I realize that it will never be so, and I am absolutely *fine* and still *fabulous* without that result. Also, God has provided me with an overabundance of what I need to thrive in this "injured" life.

It started the day I returned home from Kessler. On April 16, 2002, I came home from Kessler Institute for rehabilitation at about noon. It was an unseasonably hot day. As I entered the neighborhood, I saw that handmade posters were hung up on telephone poles. The one I remember read, "Dewey Heights is filled with joy because Jeanine is coming home!" There were balloons in the air! Neighbors with children came outside to clap and cheer!

It was a Tuesday. Parents had picked up their kids early from school; one neighbor lit up leftover firecrackers from the Fourth of July on his lawn, and another neighbor was ringing a bell and held up a poster that read, "Miracles do Happen," and depicted a rainbow.

As I turned the corner, I saw my house. Spring flowers had been planted, and a new spring wreath adorned my door. My children were waiting for me with joy-filled hugs and kisses. Neighbors came over with the same. Sub sandwiches awaited us, plentiful enough to feed the neighborhood. A "Welcome Home" cake was soon cut.

Then there was a knock at my door—my new standing wheelchair had arrived! I lost no time abandoning the manual wheelchair and jumping into my standing powerchair. When I stood up in it, everybody cheered and clapped with optimism and love.

For an afternoon, life seemed perfect. How truly blessed I am that now, as I write this in 2022, twenty years post injury have come and gone. I can honestly say that life has exceeded my greatest expectations, despite my horrific injury.

As a Christian, this should not be surprising. Scriptures from the bible have you covered in every life situation.

We are reminded in Philippians 4:6–7 (NIV), "Do not be anxious about anything; but in every situation, by prayer and petition, with thanksgiving, present your requests to God; and the peace of God, which transcends all understanding will guard your hearts and minds in Christ Jesus."

In other words, the peace and joy you will experience is far more wonderful than the human mind can understand. I am an example of promises made and promises kept. But you can't know about God's promises without seeking them out by learning about them from and through the Bible, although this book gives you a healthy start.

Today, I chose to write a different letter to my drowsy driver. This letter drips with gratitude and healing power, rather than pain:

Dear Julio,

Don't be upset or blame yourself for the car accident that occurred on November 23, 2001. You are not to blame for me suffering a spinal cord injury. The avoidable car accident created the potential for harm, but you did not seal my fate; my truck manufacturer did that.

The manufacturer chose to keep producing a known untrustworthy and irresponsibly engineered SUV that was unstable. They knew about its dangers and kept producing it anyway.

The professional safety experts I hired were certain that, had the truck been safely manufactured, it would have spun and stopped in the wrong direction on the highway, but it never would have flipped at the gentle speed of fifteen miles per hour.

God and his guardian angels had my back. They planted a police car right behind me on that fateful day. The police officer would have protected me from oncoming traffic. The hired safety experts assured me that I would have walked away from that accident.

I totally forgive you and remove you as the cause of my injury and want you to understand how God used my injury to bless my life:

- I was able to stay home and give my "all" to my children, who are now very successful, well-adjusted overachievers.
- I had the personal time to dedicate myself to a Bible study that lasted almost a decade.
- Tom and I had the means to fund an in vitro procedure, allowing my nephew and his beautiful wife to conceive a son and, later, a daughter.
- I had time to dedicate myself to many worthwhile charities, adding depth and richness to my life.
- Tom and I had the means to offer our children the best education money can buy.
- Tom and I had the means to buy a two-week time share in St. John, USVI. Over the years, dozens upon dozens of our friends and family members have joined us for some great vacations and will continue to do so for years to come.
- I had the time and blessings to publish a book so my story might not have to die with me; it, God willing, might reach and inspire those chosen by God to receive spiritual guidance.

As I finish this book in 2023, how blessed I am to be able to write that twenty injured years have come and gone, and despite my horrific injury, life has exceeded my greatest expectations! As a Christian, I should not be surprised. Scriptures from the New Testament predict this outcome:

Jesus said to his disciples, "'Have faith in God.' Jesus answered. 'Truly I tell you—if anyone says to this mountain, "Go throw yourself into the sea" and does not doubt in his heart, but believes what they say will happen, it will be done for them. Therefore, I tell you, whatever you ask for in prayer, believe that you have received it, and it will be yours. And when you stand praying if you hold anything against anyone, forgive them, so that your Father in Heaven may forgive you your sins'" (Mark 11:22–25, NIV).

"Jesus said, 'Ask and it will be given to you; seek and you will find knock and it will be opened to you. For everyone who asks, receives, and the one who seeks, finds and to the one who knocks, the door will be opened. Which of you, if a son asks for bread, will give him a stone? Or if he asks for a fish, will give him a snake?'" (Matthew 7:7–10: NIV).

"Jesus said, 'If you remain in me, and my words remain in you, ask whatever you wish and it will be done for you'" (John 15:7, NIV).

There are many more verses like these, among them Philippians 4:6–8, James 4:3, and John 14:13–14. I have chosen to include my favorites from the New Testament here because they have personally helped me to heal on an emotional level.

Chapter 13

2016 Highlights

More miracles and blessings occurred in 2016, which continued to reinforce and augment my faith in God. This year promised to be a financially challenging one, despite my good fortunes of the past. Beginning in September 2016, I had three children in college at the same time. The tuition was already put aside. What was not accounted for was their spending money for books, food, gas, and incidentals, which can really add up, especially if their semesters were too academically demanding for them to work for money.

In an attempt to remain proactive and get ready for "what may come," I flipped a house and got a job! Here was another way for me to *rise to the occasion*, which, for me, has always been a promoter of self-love and respect.

Two of my ICU nurses from 2001 are still friends of mine. Naomi and her husband, Jim, have been to the Caribbean with us twice. Taryn and Seth have partaken in different dates out to dinner, or Taryn and I have enjoyed many a breakfast together over the years.

One afternoon, Taryn and her contractor approached me about being a partner in flipping houses. I quickly accepted for a few reasons—there were three of us, making purchasing the house rather affordable. I felt that the risk of losing money was greatly diminished because one of the investors was also the contractor. The quicker he could finish the improvements on the house, the greater the profit.

So, I accepted the offer and remained quite optimistic that the result would be a lucrative one.

The house was ready to put on the market by the third month of our ownership. Our biggest obstacle was not finding a buyer; that proved to be easy. What we were not expecting was the strict lending criteria of the banks. The banks had been too liberal in years past. They had approved loans that had set their customers up to fail financially, and now our flip team would pay the price.

After ten months and three other prospective buyers, we were able to close the deal. We made a tiny profit. But to me, personally, it was not worth the stress of having such a tight cash flow. Consequently, I did not continue flipping houses, although countless people who chose this path have met success.

Instead, I was contacted by the Nursing Staff at Kessler Institute for Rehabilitation. They claimed that I would be the "perfect fit" for a job they had posted and invited me to interview for it. The management interviewed me to be the next New Jersey director of ThinkFirst. ThinkFirst is a national injury prevention organization. Every state has a director, who would ask victims of spinal cord and traumatic brain injuries to tell their stories of how their injuries might have been avoided had they put *thinking first* into action.

The audiences of this program would be school children of all ages—from elementary school through high school seniors. My job would be to contact schools, informing them of this *free* program, which did seem to be tailor-made for me. I knew many teachers in many schools, which would give me an advantage when it came to booking schools.

I also knew a lot of people whose injuries might have been prevented had they *not* been drinking before driving or texting while driving or had they been wearing their bike helmet. Or a *big common mistake* still is diving into the waves at the beach! This is a major cause of young teens breaking their necks. *Go in feet first, never head first.*

Finally, for me, the biggest factor in accepting the job was that I did *not* have to ask for money! This program was free to all schools as this was Kessler's way of giving back to the community. Kessler would pay my speakers good money as they tried to prevent "invincible" youths from causing harmful injuries to themselves or others. It was a win–win for all involved!

My speakers are referred to as VIPs in this program. At first, I chuckled to myself—VIP, hmm, very important person or very injured person? The real answer was fantastic. My VIPs stood for voices for injury prevention—*brilliant*!

For two years, I was able to build up the program, because I got to know so many great VIPs, who I trained, incorporating my teaching skills into improving their presentations. The communication skills I valued were always successful in reaching young people.

Kessler hired me to manage and schedule VIPs, but they did not want me not to *become* a VIP. I was not a good candidate to speak to teens about my story, because I had no fault in my accident, *and* I had been wearing a seat belt.

The only thing I could have done, was to check the safety reports on my SUV, which were very *unfavorable*. Ironically, I had bought my SUV to be safer, as I was now a mom and, most often, transporting "precious cargo."

I did return more than once to the two schools where I had previously taught, Middletown High School North and JFK High School in Iselin, which is where I was teaching up until the day of my accident. I advised young drivers to look up and heed the safety reports of every vehicle they are considering to buy or drive. Make sure that the vehicle is crashworthy with a strong roof.

Within two years, I was given other jobs within my original job. ThinkFirst also sponsors a "fall prevention" class for senior citizens, which requires me to contact senior centers and assisted living facilities. The classes were super easy to book because they are *free*, and these institutions employ "activity directors" to come up with activities to entertain their members. My phone call reaching out to activity directors made their day! I was offering an easy activity that *always* fit into their tight budgets.

My third new responsibility was tailor-made for me as well. Patients at Kessler suffering from a SCI are strongly encouraged to take five classes before returning home. It's part of our Lunch and Learn Series. The classes include Introduction to SCI, Bowel Management, Skin Management, Bladder Management, and Transitioning Home. I teach two of the five classes.

Finally, I saved the best part of my job for last. This is the volunteer portion of my work. I am a peer counselor. This means I am paired up with an inpatient who has a similar injury to mine. With the patients' permission, I act as their mentor to SCI, helping them to *catapult* themselves back to a life that is great again. I am able to offer them hope very early on that their life will be *great* again. I ask patients what their first priority goals are for each month, and I help them reach their goals. For me, that part of the job is the pleasure of my life.

Chapter 14

2017 Highlights

My oldest son, Steven, graduated from Rochester Institute of Technology in December 2016 with a BS in computer systems and forensics. That's a fancy title for cybersecurity, a hot promising and lucrative field. Steven got a well-paying job right away and asked for a party to celebrate. I quickly agreed and got very busy planning a party. What I did not do was seek out God's will and blessing.

I booked a party an hour south of us at a banquet hall that was owned by friends who we consider to be family. We chose the catering menu and chose a DJ and the latest date in January before the spring semester would begin so that as many cousins and friends of Steven's who were still in college, would be able to attend the party. I then ordered invitations and sent them all out.

Then this guilt and shame came over me. The message I got loud and clear was: *How hypocritical*! Your charity that you claim to love is all about helping the poor. You should be giving the dollars it costs to fund the party to the poor. Steven doesn't need for anything, yet you still want more. Shame on you!

I could not shake my guilt and confided in Steven. He looked at it much differently than I had. He communicated that, with my mindset, he was being punished for not being poor or, as he put it, for being successful.

I understood his point of view, but I still could not shake the weight in my chest, which I equated with guilt. I called my friend who is a priest as well as a biblical scholar. I explained to Father Nick everything I have explained here. He said some very complimentary things about me that I am not comfortable repeating, especially since I do not agree with his assessment. He also said that he didn't want to get in between my God and me but that he didn't agree with my thoughts here.

He dove into Jesus's behavioral examples set forth during his lifetime. "Jeanine, as you remember, Jesus was attending a wedding when the host ran out of wine. His mother insisted that Jesus save the host from shame and embarrassment by rectifying the situation. She ordered the servants to fill the empty wine jugs with water. Jesus took the water jugs and transformed the water into *fine wine*, even though it was customary and cultural to save the inferior quality wine for last because few would notice (John 2:1–11).

Father then reminded me about the woman who rubbed very expensive perfume on Jesus's feet. She was rebuked by Judas Iscariot, who criticized her for not selling the perfume and using the money to feed the poor instead. Jesus defended her actions by saying, "Leave her alone, it was intended that she should keep this perfume for the day of my burial. You will always have the poor among you, but you will not always have me" (John 12:3–8, NIV). Father explained that Jesus endorsed splurging at opportune times.

I decided to go through with the party plans despite the warning signs I had received but did not heed. The results spoke for themselves. In New Jersey, there was one snowstorm that year. It snowed like a blizzard on the day of the party—from about noon until 9:00 p.m. Eighty people were invited to the party, and about twenty-four people braved the storm and made the party that night. I believe to this day that the storm was my punishment for not listening to my God, who only wants the best for His people. The money spent that night would have been better spent to serve God's poor, not on my son, who had always been given the best life has to offer. Father Nick does not agree with my analysis. The two undisputable facts are 1: The minute I finalized my plans for the party with a payment, my heart became heavy. 2: The night did not turn out nearly as planned.

I found my Colombian family!

"What?" you might ask. "I am almost done with this book and you have not mentioned *anything* about having family in Colombia!"

Well, you are correct, my friend. So, let's dive into this story, which should not disappoint.

When I was in high school, I decided I really wanted to become fluent in Spanish. To my disappointment, studying it in school would not be enough to meet that goal. I would somehow have to immerse myself in the language for a few months. I decided I could go to Mexico and be a nanny for a family. By communicating with the kids all summer, I could improve significantly. I shared this idea with my Spanish teacher, and he was not happy with my plan; he did not think it held enough fun for me.

The very next day, Mr. C came to visit me in gym class with the following proposition: "I know a family who lives in Medellin, Colombia. This family has two girls your age who want to improve their English. Would you want to have an exchange program with them? They would come here and study with you, and then you could go there and study with them."

I didn't have to think about it. I replied, "I would have to ask my parents, first. But I would love that."

This was my junior year of high school, and my mother saw the value in the exchange right away and agreed just about as quickly as I had. Before I knew it, friends of the Colombian family who were in New York on business were at my house for dinner hoping to meet us and send a full scouting report back to the student exchange family to say "yay" or "nay" to the impending unofficial student exchange program.

Much sooner than later, our family was welcoming Maria, twenty-one, to our home and way of life! We had a great time, and time flew as usual. By the time senior year rolled around, I had tickets to spend an entire summer after high school graduation as a Marymount student in Medellin.

When I arrived on July 5, 1982, Maria was working full-time and realized she couldn't offer me the great time she had hoped. So, I was transferred to a cousin's house and had the experience of a lifetime. I studied at school during the week as did the girls, and we spent weekends at their country house. What amazed me was how both houses were fully staffed with a maid and cook and, in the country, a landscaper. The father employed a chauffeur, and the parents had much more time for fun than my family. It was uplifting to see a family so happy, with virtually no problems to speak of, or at least when you compared their living situation to ours.

By the end of the summer, I could speak Spanish without translating every word from English to Spanish in my mind first. I was able to automatically speak Spanish. Those of you learning a second language can understand the scope of this great accomplishment.

When I started my freshman year at Montclair State College, it was understood that, come December 1982, my two Colombian sisters would study here. They would attend my former high school during the week, and I would be home between semesters until January 13. After that, I would come home over the weekends to hang out with my Colombian sisters. They spoke English quite well.

When they returned to Colombia, we soon lost touch, much to my chagrin. When Facebook became a thing, I purposely joined immediately, with the hope of finding my Colombian family again. I missed everyone so much and always credited them with giving me the confidence to become a Spanish teacher. The Spanish immersion summer experience of 1982 improved my ability to speak to the point where my confidence level motivated me to pursue and graduate with a BA in Spanish and education from Rutgers University in December 1986.

I also studied for six weeks in Salamanca, Spain, during the summer of '85 through a second immersion program. This was an official university-sponsored program, where I traveled with a group of forty college juniors and a three-women group of graduate students. Although I improved and learned from this program, it did not compare to the love shared between me and my Colombian family, who remained near and dear to my heart for decades later.

I tried to locate this family by searching for them on Facebook but to no avail. I left my maiden name attached before my married one in the hope they might someday reach out to me.

As I was paying my bills on Holy Thursday of 2017, an overwhelming desire overcame me in an instant. I had a divine craving, an enormous urge to look up my family on Facebook using a different last name than the one I had used in my previous searches.

I had a hit and clicked on the name. there was the picture—the parents, their three children, the children and spouses of each minus one significant other (he must have been taking the picture), and Tia! Aunt Maria Teresa had always been with them then, and she was still with them now. Her presence sealed my confidence that this was my family. And I could not *wait* to reach out to them!

I immediately tagged them on Messenger and explained that I had *finally* found them after a seven-year Facebook search. My computer started ringing and dinging as the messages just kept coming, one after another after another, from the mom and the two girls and the aunt. Everyone was so excited.

And then the first girl to come and visit from Medellin called me, and my Spanish never faded. After fifteen years of teaching Spanish grammar, my irregular verbs stayed accurately irregular, and my vocabulary stood by my side. My speed was not quite up to par, but it didn't matter. I was understandable and euphoric.

Tom sensed my excitement and caught some as well. Before I knew it, Tom, Tommy, and I had bought three roundtrip tickets to Medellin, Colombia, from August 1 through August 12, 2017.

The reunion was one of the great highlights of my life. My Colombian family and I keep in touch via text messages, face-to-face phone calls, and WhatsApp. The mom and aunt have visited us twice more since our trip of 2017.

Chapter 15

2018 Highlights

My Colombian family's youngest daughter was like a sister to me. Ana was exuberant, very spiritual, and a fantastic mom. She asked if her eldest son, Miguel or "Migue", could come and visit us to improve his English. I wholeheartedly accepted his visit, and I began studying great places to visit in Manhattan so I could confidently take Migue to see its main attractions by train, bus and ferry.

He could only stay twelve days because he had been accepted into a very prestigious music school in Medellin and scheduled his trip from right after Christmas to the first week of January. I felt very happy because, despite the bitter cold, we went into the city seven days out of the twelve.

My children got to meet him and show him around some favorite sights that were nearest and dearest to them. Miguel was very appreciative of his trip, and my youngest son was ready to spend his spring semester of his junior year of college in Barcelona, Spain.

I am including this paragraph in with the year's greatest blessings because what mother would not be thrilled with her son studying abroad in Barcelona with the world at his fingertips? As it turned out, Tommy only had classes three days a week and was able to travel the other four days. Tommy realized that, once he was in Europe, air travel to other European countries was very inexpensive, as was their Metro System. As a result, Tommy visited about ten countries and forty cities while studying in Barcelona. This, along with his high school travel experience to France and Spain and a college freshman study program in Japan, has made my son a world traveler at the young age of just twenty-one.

I credit my wheelchair for this blessing; it created a way to receive extra funding, enabling me to enroll Tommy in RISD, a very prominent but expensive art college in Providence, Rhode Island.

My daughter was able to embrace her first choice in universities as well, also one of the most expensive, which was Loyola University in Baltimore, Maryland. Marisa graduated magna cum laude with a degree in biology and psychology. She planned on going to grad school. Right out of Loyola, she got a job managing an office for two physical therapists. She became certified as a physical trainer and Les Mills instructor of Body Combat and Body Pump.

Tommy followed right in her footsteps and got the proper training and licensing for Body Pump and Body Combat as well. He started teaching fitness at Brown University, which was located right next to Rhode Island School of Design, his undergrad school of choice. My husband Tom and I used to say that our youngest son was an instructor at Brown University.

Chapter 16

2020 Highlights

As we all know, 2020 will go down in history as the year that COVID-19 shut down the world. Everyone was in hibernation. The coronavirus started killing people by the hundreds all across the globe, putting forth proof that it really is a small world. For good reason, the world became "germophobic," and streets remained desolate; hundreds and hundreds of small business owners shut their doors, never to open them again.

I needed to put my will to the test once again. As long as I stay productive, I will *thrive*! And thrive I have. I decided to write this book and threw myself into writing it. God has awoken me on plenty of nights with specific instructions on what to include, messages to add, and events to remember. It has been a deeply spiritual experience. The burning question still remains. When the momentum from my ride has been exhausted and its effect no longer impacts you as a reader, will you still be motivated and humbled enough to make changes in your life to create a more spiritually-elevated you?

Tom and I also refurbished our upstairs with new hardwood floors, new carpeting in our children's rooms, and new mattresses and fresh paint that was lighter and brighter to lift the mood of a promising new decade.

I was motivated to update the upstairs because my Colombian family wanted to come and visit. All of my children were very excited at the thought of meeting everyone they had heard so much about.

Unfortunately, COVID 19 shut down the world. Life as we knew it came to a screeching halt. Most people worked from home, but many others simply lost their jobs because of lack of business. Millions of people, who were usually out and about supporting local small businesses, were shut down in their homes, afraid of catching COVID, because it had taken so many people's lives.

My children all moved home because they were all working virtually and wanted to save money by not spending money on rent. They were all deeply grateful that they had never accumulated any college debt, like most people their age had accrued. They did learn, however, that, when you are just starting out in a career and paying rent, it is extremely hard to save money. So, their childhood bedrooms that had become luxurious guest rooms just the week before, were once again flipped back into the children's bedrooms. I chuckled to myself knowing that, the laugh was on me, thinking once again, that "I" was in control.

I found some blessings from the global pandemic. My beloved children were all back home. I had poured my heart and soul into raising all three of them. The truth that I quickly realized was that they were great human beings that I loved to be around. Their company elevated my soul. My fast-paced life slowed down for me. I was very grateful to have enough time and much reduced stress to be able to effortlessly smell the roses and live my blessings like never before.

Feeling blessed is wonderful and one of the attributes of remaining happy. Another ingredient to maintaining happiness through my living experiences is to give back. For example: Early on in my injury, in Spring of 2003, I learned that the daughter of my mom's best friend was in the hospital. I dropped in to see Denise and my mom's friend, Barbara was also there right by her daughter's side as I had hoped. They were surprised and happy to see me. I didn't know what was wrong with Denise, but it was clear that her two boys, eight and twelve and husband had to get by often because Denise was hospitalized often for many days at a time. I decided to give back by honoring my neighbors who had cooked for me for seven months. I was only one person, but on the three days a week that her boys had baseball practice, I decided to drop off a homemade meal for the boys after school so that the dad wouldn't have to worry about dinner. The boys could come home, complete homework and then go to their practice or game. Afterwards, they would have dinner awaiting them.

Tom and I increased our charity work at our church. Tom became the lead "Minister of Hospitality" which was the Head Usher for 10:30, our preferred Mass time. He was also required to schedule all ushers to cover extra masses added for Christmas and Easter. We also became "Chairmen of Hospitality" at our annual church carnival, our biggest fundraiser. We were responsible for making sure that all volunteers were well fed during their four hours of volunteer shifts. This was a huge undertaking. This involved getting $1000 from the carnival committee in advance. I would go to Sam's Club and buy most things in bulk such as: Ziplock bags, cookies, chips, pretzels, cheese doodles, cold cuts, tuna fish, packets of mayo, mustard, ketchup, sugar, creamer, coffee, iced tea peanut butter, jelly, hot and cold cups and bread. I would pack up the car from Sam's and take everything to the carnival. We would direct volunteers to pack snacks and make sandwiches. Another group of volunteers would run the food out to volunteers so that while they worked at their volunteer stands, they would be well fed. Tom and I would be at the carnival in our garage stand every waking minute of the carnival. We did this for ten years. The monies earned from this fundraiser would fund our 85 outreach ministries.

For the past 15 years, I have been the Intake Manager of a ministry that is nearest and dearest to my heart...The St. Vincent de Paul Society of St. Matthias. This ministry helps people who are experiencing a financial hardship keep their rent paid and lights on. We personally interview each and every household needing our help. We interview in person, at the home of the clients who request our services. Since I am unable to access most homes, my contribution is to work the hotline. I call people back who have left messages for us, to make sure that they qualify for our help and entering them in our database, giving them a case number to protect their identity and to assign them a Case Manager to interview them when one becomes available. For me, this ministry is extremely rewarding. At the end of each year, we have helped dozens upon dozens of people in our community including extra food during Christmas, Thanksgiving and Easter. We are just one ministry of 85 trying to "give back" to our community.

Finally, I have saved my favorite story for last. This true story contains my favorite miracle of all. My two older brothers, Tommy and Eddie, along with their wives, blessed us with four boys, all unique and very special. I became a very proud Aunt at just 10 years young. During my entire lifetime, I tried to be a good Aunt by staying active in their lives. This was rather easy, until Eddie, his wife Vivian and two boys moved to Florida. I did the best I could from a far distance.

Michael or "Mike" was Ed's youngest and, as a young teenager, started making unwise choices. By the time he was 16 he was famous in Southern Florida for all the wrong reasons. He ended up being incarcerated for gang violence early on and then for distributing drugs in his adult life and serving a separate much longer sentence as an adult. Mike, like his father became an alcoholic and later, unlike his dad became a drug addict. He gave his family much heartache as you can imagine. Eddie would call me often, expressing his disappointment and, at times extreme sadness because he had zero confidence that life would get better for his very troubled son. While Mike was in prison, Tom and I flew down to attend my other nephew's wedding. Ed, Eddie's oldest, was getting married to Tara. Much to everyone's extreme disappointment, my brother Eddie couldn't attend his son's wedding. He became very sick due to alcoholism. Everyone got along with my brother very well, as long as you did not acknowledge his drinking. He never admitted that he drank at all, not even occasionally. He never admitted he ever had a problem. He never attempted to get help of any kind. He never even admitted he drank alcohol to his doctors when they would question him.

Sadly, by the time Mike was released from prison, my brother had only a few weeks to be reunited with his son before he died in his sleep in 2010 at the young age of 59. He did live long enough to meet and hold his first grandson Dean, born to Ed and Tara Senerote.

Once out of prison, Mike started struggling with his addictions once again. By the third inpatient rehab, life started improving for Mike because he started making better decisions. His third attempt at remaining clean and sober was working. I credit this to his amazing girlfriend, now wife Brittany. She had enough self-love and respect needed to make the tough choice of taking all of her belongings from Mike's house, calling on her strong brothers to arrive while Mike was "working" and help her pack up the house and move back to her childhood home in Buffalo NY. When Mike came home, his house was empty and Brittany was nowhere to be found. This was Mike's "rock bottom" and his motivation to finally get in control of his life.

Mike gets the break he needs to turn his life around. He convinces the owner of a construction company to take a chance on him. This construction owner is eager to find competent people to install windows. Mike is an expert in many areas of construction, window installation being among his areas of expertise. His boss is quickly impressed. Not only does Mike have a strong work ethic rarely seen today, but he does a great job executing his installations and his customers are raving about the end result.

We now fast forward to 2018 when the foundation for my favorite miracle is promised. A few years have passed and Mike has remained clean and sober. He has been promoted by the owner of his company and together with Brittany are planning to get married. Life is looking great until Brittany called me sobbing from her own hospital bed.

Brittany had only one fallopian tube left. She was counting on that one fallopian tube to carry out her dreams of having children. She was forced to have one removed two years earlier due to a few ectopic pregnancies. It was now apparent that her one and only remaining tube would have to be removed as well due to a fourth ectopic pregnancy that was threatening her life. Her dreams of becoming a mom were just crushed, and her anguish was understood. I quickly tried to "fix" the problem by offering a solution. "Brittany, there are more ways of becoming a mom. You could adopt a baby. She continued to sob, "I can't…Mike's a Felon!" I pitched another ball to home plate, "Okay, well you can foster a child then" hoping for a home run. "I can't, Brittany continued, Mike's a felon!" "There's always invitro," I pleaded. She answered through her sobs, "We could never afford that procedure. I have researched it." "How much is it?" I asked. When she told me, I said, "Well, I can afford it and you have my word that I will fund an invitro for you" Brittany did not see that coming and she was extremely appreciative. My immediate fulfillment was that she was able to enter the operating room knowing that she still had the realistic hope of becoming a "mama" one day. What I did not realize then, was that my beautiful niece worked for an infertility specialist, a Doctor who specialized in a very specific and successful approach to invitro fertilization.

People I spoke with along the way tried to discourage me by saying that there is no guarantee that it will work on the first try. Right after my promise to Brittany, I had a dream that Mike and Brittany would conceive a boy and he is destined for greatness. I believe that this whole situation was blessed by God. Further validation occurred which reinforced this belief. Tom found a life insurance policy that had cash built into it that could be withdrawn and not be paid back!! God was behind this plan from the beginning. I based my promise on my investments, but ended up being blessed by found money that had very little tax consequences. We withdrew all available cash, funded a much-needed new roof over our heads *and* a baby!!

Santino was born in 2020, followed by a sister named Stella in 2022! First there were two and now there are four! I am the proud Godmother to Santino and so proud of Mike who has now been promoted to the sales department of his company. He now sells the windows he used to install. For the first time in his life, he works his brain harder than his body. He is such a great hands-on Dad and husband. Brittany is a very loving mom and her children will thrive. My sister-in-law Vivian is best thing that ever happened to my brother Eddie and her dedication to her children has never wavered. The love she has for her three grandchildren knows no limits. She loves her family whole-heartedly. She is the oldest of her three siblings and is the glue that holds everyone together. She always has the makings for a homemade meal at her fingertips. She is an exceptionally hard worker and loving Nana. She just turned 70 and never stops and never naps. She says that her body will have plenty of time to rest when she's dead!

Chapter 17

A Tribute to Tom

I have plenty to say about my wonderful man, my husband of over thirty years, who made the conscious decision to stick by his original marriage vows of taking care of me through the good, bad, and ugly times; in sickness and in health' through richer or poorer; and until death shall we part.

He stuck with me through thick and thin. According to Adrienne Asch, a professor of biology, ethics, and human reproduction at Wellesley College and a past president of the Society of Disability Studies, "The data are that marriages do break up more often when there is a disability than when there isn't. We also know that men leave wives more often than wives leave husbands."

"There are many reasons for this. When one income is lost, and there is a decrease in household income, much stress on both partners can be created, increasing stress on the marriage as a whole." Asch goes on to explain, "very often, the injured person has a detrimental personality change, making the injured person a completely different partner than the husband or wife signed up for."

I thank God for this one. I am not physically the same person, but mentally, spiritually, personality wise, and intellectually, I am the same person Tom married. Things have not always been easy, but we have each decided that the other person is worth the effort.

"Because You Loved Me" sung by Celine Dion, is a song that

sums up my gratitude for two very important beings in my life—God Almighty and my beloved husband Tom.

To my God and to my husband, I cannot think of better words of gratitude. "I love you" leaves me unsatisfied. My gratitude is eternal.

"Because You Loved Me,"
with lyrics by Diane Warren:

For all those times you stood by me
For all the truth that you made me see
For all the joy you brought to my life
For all the wrong that you made right
For every dream you made come true
For all the love I found in you
I'll be forever thankful baby
You're the one who held me up
Never let me fall
You are the one who saw me through … through it all

Refrain:
You were my strength when I was weak
You were my voice when I couldn't speak
You were my eyes when I couldn't see
You saw the best there was in me
Lifted me up when I couldn't reach
You gave me faith 'cause you believed
I'm everything I am because you loved me

You gave me wings and made me fly
You touched my hand, I could touch the sky
I lost my faith, you gave it back to me
You said no star was out of reach
You stood by me, and I stood tall
I had your love; I had it all
I'm grateful for each day you gave me

Maybe I don't know that much;
but I know this much is true
I was blessed because I was loved by you

Refrain

You were always there for me
The tender wind that carried me
A light in the dark shining your love into my life
You've been my inspiration
Through the lies you were the truth
My world is a better place
Because of you

Refrain

My husband Tom has the most *amazing* memory. He remembers where things are with such detail and precision that it is hard for me, who doesn't remember what I ate for dinner the night before, not to be envious. He took one bible study forty-five years ago, but still recalls more facts and scripture locations (chapter and verse) than I can after twenty-five years of study!

Tom had a very charmed childhood, another blessing I count, because his quality of life as a youth has worked in our favor as a family.

Tom's maternal grandfather, Esteban "Chilo" Bird, graduated from the University of Pennsylvania in the late 1920s when only the very privileged went to college. After receiving a prestigious BA in business, he went on to earn a master's degree at the Wharton School of Business. He owned three yachts in his lifetime and became an avid sports fisherman in the '50s. He founded the San Juan Club Nautico, and its fishing tournaments still happen today. Chilo was known for catching dozens of marlins and swordfish, and his catches broke records frequently within the tournaments. To this day, his bust still exists in the San Juan Harbor Club Marina.

Even though Esteban "Chilo" Bird lived in Puerto Rico, he visited his daughter Blanquita every chance he had in New Jersey, and there were many slides taken as evidence of these trips.

Tom's mom was a high school Spanish teacher who went to the best schools herself in the '40's, as her father valued education very highly. She had all her summers off and would travel with all of her children in tow to Villa Caparra, Puerto Rico, where she was born and raised.

During her eight weeks of summer, Chilo would rent a house in St. John, USVI, right on the shore of Caneel Bay for one month. His colleague was the owner of the house, so he was always able to rent it. For seven years, Tom had the privilege of sailing the crystal blue waters of the Caribbean, fishing, swimming, and snorkeling.

His dad, Cart T. Valenti, was an attorney, a Villanova Graduate who was able to join his family for two weeks in St. John every summer. When we view these beautiful slides, it occurs to me how blessed my husband and my brother-in-law and sisters-in-law were to be vacationing two months every year, beginning in Puerto Rico and ending in St. John. The love of the Caribbean and love of fishing and boating was in my husband's blood. "Papi", who died when Tom was seven, will always hold a very extra special place in Tom's heart.

I met Tom on that fateful day when his mom, my cooperating Spanish teacher, Blanquita Bird Valenti, invited me to her home for dinner and sat me down to Tom's immediate left. Tom had to eat and run because he taught a boating course at Middlesex County College. One of the things I learned about Tom that night was that he had bought his first boat before he bought his first car! He had graduated the year before from the University of Colorado with a degree in civil engineering.

Within the next two weeks, Blanquita invited me to see *Man of La Mancha* at a local county playhouse. Of course, I accepted without knowing anything else. Nothing else mattered. I loved Blanquita's company any way I could get it. I met her at her house in New Brunswick, and we took Blanquita's car to see the play.

As it turned out, Blanquita and Carl sat in the front seat. In the very wide back seat sat Mary, their oldest daughter, with her boyfriend Richie. Next to Richie sat Tom!

The play was great, and Tom and I had a lot to talk about. And talk we did. When the play was over, he told his mom he would take me to a local restaurant for a drink, and Mary and Richie came with us. I took that to be a first date.

Our second date was on a Saturday, with Mary and Richie again. But it was fishing on Tom's boat. I had never gone fishing, and I had never gone boating. In retrospect, I dressed too nicely for a very casual occasion, but I knew enough to wear a bathing suit under my clothes. By the afternoon, my long pants came off. I was wearing a bikini that I felt comfortable wearing only because I had just finished drinking my second beer.

Then it hit me. I had to go to the bathroom. The *bathroom*! Where was it? I had not thought about it before, but there was no bathroom. I was on an eighteen-foot StarCraft with two outboard motors and two bench seats, the basic and bare necessities needed to fish.

I noticed the cooler containing our lunches and a smaller tackle box containing live bait and plastic paraphernalia that was supposed to trick fish into thinking there was food at the end of a fishing rod.

The only other thing was a white bucket. Could that be the poor excuse for a toilet? I was *mortified*! Not only did I have to sit on a bucket in front of two men I hardly knew, but there were other boats *all around me*! And it was *me* I was thinking of—the same me who closed the bathroom door and locked it when I was home alone! How was I going to pee in a bucket in front of a crowd?

Well, my kidneys did not have the answer either. I sat on that bucket, with my bikini bottom crotch pulled to the side, and my kidneys became *very* shy. *I couldn't go!* I had to pee so badly I was in pain. But I could not go.

What was worse than the embarrassment of using the bucket once? Having to explain that your kidneys were shy and you would have to ask a second time as they turned their backs to you to give you privacy.

My kidneys finally surrendered, and I was, at last, able to relieve myself.

I was very seasick that day. And when Tom handed me the tuna sub that had appealed to me on land, I don't know how I didn't lose my cookies. Somehow, I managed not to get sick. More proof that there is a God and he was working for me!

Our first full date did not go so badly, because there was another one, followed by another one. We got married four years later. In preparation for the celebration, he asked if he could choose the honeymoon destination. He said he knew a most special place and he wanted to take me there.

We picked a wedding date of July 20,1991, because, as a teacher, I had the summers off and could enjoy the final preparations with little stress. A second advantage to securing that date was that, upon returning from a two-week honeymoon, I would still have a month to enjoy being a newlywed before returning to work. Teaching was a career I loved. But once the school year started, a teacher's job is *never* done until the end of June.

We had a glorious first week of our honeymoon, split between Caneel Bay; St. John, USVI; and Little Dix Bay in Virgin Gorda, BVI. I had never been exposed to such gorgeous crystal blue waters and white sandy beaches. Caneel Bay was a gorgeous Rock Resort, originally owned by Lawrence Rockefeller, who owned the entire island of St. John. Before his death, the billionaire donated it to the government of St. John, provided that 60 percent of the island remained a national forest.

Tom could not wait to show me the house his grandfather used to rent every July until he was seven years old. It was now property of Caneel Bay and occupied by the resort's groundskeeper. This resort was beautiful, with lush gardens, beautiful bungalows, and hiking trails with breathtaking views. The quaint but vibrant downtown area boasted artisan shops filled with goods made by local artists. I was in awe of the island's natural beauty and very safe environment. I just kept asking myself the same question, "If this is St. John, what in the world is heaven like?" How could any place possibly top this?

Our second week was spent in Puerto Rico meeting a side of Tom's family I had never met, along with certain family members I had met. We stayed in one of the most beautiful hotels on the island, the Caribe Hilton. The grounds were beautiful, but the beach and water quality paled in comparison to the USVI and the BVI.

It was in Puerto Rico that I met Tom's Uncle Steve, Blanquita's brother. Like his father, Chilo, Steve was a yachtsman, an avid sports fisherman, and a very successful civil engineer. He was president and owner of Bird Construction, a major commercial builder of the downtown area of San Juan. As a wedding gift, he let us use his yacht with a complete crew for a day. Tom wanted to go fishing. The seventy-five-foot yacht was gorgeous and elegant, with amenities our house didn't even have.

I would be remiss in concluding this chapter dedicated to my husband without explaining how Tom's childhood, which fostered a love of St. John, came full circle to further bless our lives.

A year before my catastrophic injury, Tom began to build an addition to our two thousand-square foot Cape Cod home. This highly anticipated event was a fulfillment of a mutual dream we had both worked hard to achieve. Tom had bought the house when he was single. His new purchase was located right across the street from the house in which he grew up. He had originally bought the neighboring house with the intention of flipping it. His brother-in-law Richie had provided the down payment, and it would be Tom's contribution to update it as quickly as possible. The hope had always been to resell it at a significant profit.

By the time Tom had finished making improvements, a year had passed, and the housing market had come crashing down. The year was 1987, making it impossible to sell the house for any type of profit. Tom believed the best solution would be to buy the house himself by assuming the mortgage and paying Richie back for the initial down payment. Tom's house had four bedrooms and two baths.

Tom asked his youngest sister, Rose, if she would like to move in as a renter with a girlfriend and pay a modest rent to help make the mortgage payment easier for Tom to afford. They eagerly accepted, and Tom's house started to make great memories while we were dating. I ended up with an additional blessing of marrying into the house.

By our third year of marriage, our family began to expand. We were blessed with three beautiful children within four years. Then, in 1999, my father accepted my offer of moving in with us after having quadruple bypass surgery and a mitral valve replacement at the age of eighty.

When he accepted my offer, I was very relieved; he lived twenty minutes away, and every time he did not answer my phone call, my imagination would run away with me. I would imagine the worst. This was before the convenience of cell phones. The only phone I could call was Dad's house phone. Whenever he did not answer my call, I could never be sure if it was because he was not home or because he was on the floor from a fall, hurt and not able to get up. After a year of asking neighbors to check in on him, I was more than ready to find a different solution.

Before he could change his mind after he had accepted the offer to live with us, I went through his house, filled an entire dumpster with Tom's help, had the house painted on the inside, and put the house up for sale.

As far as Tom and I were concerned, our house had to have an office, since both of our jobs required personal desk space. Using one bedroom as our mandatory office space was the perfect solution, leaving us with a total of three bedrooms, the perfect space for us— until Dad moved in. We were very happy to have my father with us, and we received him with open arms and bright smiles.

From that day forward, no one had their own sleeping space, which now meant that the plans we had for an addition became stronger than ever. Tom drew up the architectural plans, and we were very excited to be doubling the size of our house! By the date of my accident, the entire two thousand-square foot addition was enclosed and insulated; the twenty-foot-by-thirty-five-foot, mostly windowed great room downstairs was completed and painted; the much bigger kitchen was installed; and the powder room was roughed into the great room. The greatly expanded upstairs had just been insulated, but the sheetrock was not yet in place.

We were going from two old bathrooms to three and a half new bathrooms and from four bedrooms to six, with a master suite that included a walk-in closet. This was a dream come true, and I was grateful and ecstatic. I had a beautiful family, a wonderful career, and a beautiful home. I had a neighborhood I loved and celebrated by organizing annual block parties and entertaining neighbors, friends, and family regularly.

I always gave back by engaging in charity work and was very involved in my church. By the year 2000, I was volunteering twice a month at our local soup kitchen with my two oldest children by my side, helping to prepare and serve the meals to the needy and homeless. I also helped explain the weekly church readings to the youth during the children's Mass and I was teaching Sunday school. I then was teaching part-time after the birth of my third child. I had planned to teach full-time in 2002, once my youngest started full-day kindergarten. I continued to exercise regularly and had lots of energy which enabled me to give my best self to my family and my students.

My exceptional life came with hard work, but I felt that it was perfect.

When my accident occurred, Tom accepted help from his friends to help complete the upstairs part of the addition before I was scheduled to be discharged from Kessler. As I mentioned earlier in this memoir, my neighbors cooked for my family when I could not.

By the time I got home and found out we had a legitimate case against my car manufacturer, Tom had asked his best friend (and godfather to our youngest) to represent us.

As a "thank you" to his friends for all of their support when we needed it the most, Tom took his closest friends back to his happy place—the beautiful island of St. John. They stayed at a resort called the Westin. Tom noticed that many villas were for sale, and some of the villas were wheelchair accessible! He ended up putting a deposit on a timeshare.

When he came home, he showed me a video of our potential unit, and it looked like a dream. Since 2007, we have been going back to St. John with our children, extended family, and friends. We always have extra accommodations and have blessed countless people near and dear to us with extraordinary vacations. We have since bought a second week and can entertain even more people with our tremendous amenities, Tom's ability to captain a boat, and our desire to share our blessings with as many people as possible.

During each 1-week vacation session, we arrive on a Saturday. Saturday and Sunday are resort days.

Monday and Tuesday are boat days. We take guests to different beaches by boat; we know the best places to eat, where we tie up to a dock, disembark for lunch, and get back on the boat. We take guests to the best snorkeling spots in the USVI and the BVI. We go to Foxy's and Soggy Dollar, both resort spots are in the BVI, where we hang in the afternoon in the water and sip on cocktails in the sun. For me, it's a religious experience, proving time and time again what Benjamin Franklin once said about beer—it's "proof that there is a God and he wants us to be happy!"

Wednesday is island day. We go into Coral Bay for shopping and sightseeing in the downtown area and usually go into town for a nice dinner.

Thursday and Friday are beach days from a land perspective. We go to different beaches by car.

The second and final vacation week begins on a Saturday when we receive a whole different set of guests, and we repeat our itinerary once again.

Sometimes we take the Westin Ferry to St. Thomas and do some bargain hunting there. The scenery is gorgeous; the weather does not disappoint. Tom's childhood memories and love for his grandfather has motivated him to instill those same memories into our children. As a result, St. John will always hold endearing memories for our family.

When our children were younger, we also traveled with them to Puerto Rico; the Dominican Republic; and other states within the United States, such as Florida, Vermont, Rhode Island, Connecticut, Virginia, North Carolina, South Carolina, Tennessee, Nevada, California, New Orleans, New York frequently and Boston. We were also able to take two Caribbean cruises, adding St. Martin, the Bahamas, Nassau, and Bermuda to places we have visited.

As mentioned earlier, my initial trip to St. John and the BVIs was during my honeymoon in 1991. I have been wheelchair dependent during all subsequent trips to the islands which were made possible thanks to a husband who is resourceful and has never given up on his wife. Every annual trip since 2007 has been wonderful, but only *one* of those 16 trips has been miraculous.

As always, we were taking extra guests with us to enjoy another "St. John Experience." But never did I expect the experience to start out as it did.

In 2011, both of my sons were able to take their very best friend to St. John with us. Tommy's dearest friend, Sal, was also a neighbor, born six weeks after Tommy. His family had lived catty-corner from us in the Dewey Heights section of New Brunswick. He had been to Florida and Mexico but never the Caribbean. Steven's best friend, Eric, had lived a very sheltered upbringing and had only been outside of New Jersey once in his life for a school-sponsored event in Washington, DC.

We could not wait to expose Eric to our happy place, and our enthusiasm was fueled by Eric's sheer excitement. He began talking about our upcoming vacation for months before, and my excitement to bring him prevented me from sleeping well the night before our departure. We had to wake up at 5:00 a.m. for the first flight out of Newark International Airport scheduled for a 7:30 departure.

As we pulled into the parking garage of the airport, Marisa became violently ill and started vomiting in the car and fell into a sleeplike state, where she could communicate, but you really had to talk loudly and shake her for a response. I recognized the problem. She'd had this happen twice before, only to be told after every test result came back negative, that she was dehydrated. I never believed that diagnosis for a rapid second.

We called 9-1-1 and explained our location. Eric looked at me, and I could read his eyes. He was sure this dream trip would end before it even started. I quickly evaluated the situation. My husband was driving. He could disconnect the real driver's seat and put it loose behind me, and I would be able to lock into my EZ Lock located on the driver's side floor and drive to the hospital.

I got a clear divine message: "I will take care of you." It came through loudly, and my courage level skyrocketed.

"Tom, you go with everyone on vacation as planned. Marisa and I will meet you in St. John tomorrow," I demanded with all of the confidence I could muster up. I did not want to disappoint our guests, and I knew God had my back because he always has my heart.

Tom was torn. He left most of his heart with us, but I took my suitcase out of the trunk, and Tom took everyone else with him along with all the luggage and kissed us goodbye. I told him not to worry and that I would keep him informed. I put my luggage back in the car, took my place behind the wheel and headed off to Beth Israel, thanks to my GPS.

The ambulance had already left. I knew where they were taking her. I had never used this hospital before, but it had a great reputation.

When I pulled into the ER parking lot, I found an idle EMT sitting in a vacant ambulance. I rolled down my driver's window, and he followed my lead and responded in kind.

"Excuse me, sir," I said. "Can you help me? I drive from a wheelchair and cannot exit this van unless the chair behind me gets moved."

Of course, he was happy to help me and responded immediately but first gave me a special place to park—right outside the emergency room. I was extremely relieved to have such an easy parking space that I would be able to find later without any effort. I personally abhor parking garages. Had this compassionate EMT not given me this beautiful parking spot, I would have been forced into parking in an unfamiliar parking garage that would have overwhelmed me even more.

It was 6:30 a.m. and the ER was not busy. Marisa had the staff's full attention, but she could not communicate well, so I took over. Let the miracles begin! I explained that we were about to get on a plane to St. Thomas in route to St. John. The young ER Doctor said, "I lived in St. John for the past 2 years. I just got back and and I am feeling your pain!" I said, "Thanks but please know that this has happened twice before." I named each test he would prescribe to figure out a diagnosis, and he agreed with me. I also said that she presented symptoms of someone who had overdosed on some kind of drug. "I will tell you that she does not take drugs," I added. "But you are trained not to listen to Mom, because moms are often the last to know about drug abuse among their children."

The doctor agreed with me again.

I said, "Do what you must, but know that every test I described to you will come back negative. What I am demanding is that you not diagnose her as 'dehydrated.' It is more than that."

He went through every test. All results were negative.

I told him that, in 2007, Marisa was diagnosed with absence epilepsy because she would have split-second blackouts, resulting in her dropping whatever she happened to be holding.

The doctor's eyes lit up. "You are in luck! Our pediatric neurologist just got back from a two-week vacation and came in this morning, on his day off, to get ahead of his paperwork so he can start his work week all caught up."

I looked at my watch. It was only 7:30 a.m. on a Saturday morning. What a rare chance of having a neurologist of his caliber in the hospital at this time. I smiled as I remembered God's message to me: "I will take care of you."

A short time later, the neurologist came to meet me. He said, "I am sure I know what is happening with your daughter. She has transitioned from absence epilepsy to a stronger type as she has gotten older. The bad news may be that she will not grow out of her epilepsy, but the good news is that I know how to treat it. I am going to witness her EEG. I will know if I am correct by viewing the results as they happen. If she has this adult form of epilepsy, I will prescribe another drug called Keppra. And if you promise to get it filled today, I will clear you to take the first flight out to St. John tomorrow."

I remained cautiously optimistic.

The technicians set her up with many leads connected to her

scalp, trying to avoid her long hair. From previous experience I knew that with Marisa, the test preparation would take about forty-five minutes to complete. Meanwhile, my mind started to wander. What if Marisa was seriously ill and was hospitalized for a week--what would I have done? My only caregivers are Tom or Marisa. I remain unable to undress myself for bed or transfer myself from my power chair to my bed or get dressed in the morning and transfer myself independently back into my power chair from the bed. At night, I shower independently, but I cannot transfer myself into my shower chair. Because I got the message, "I will take care of you", I was distracted from worry and just did what the situation dictated. Now that I am navigating on my own and the neurologist is confident he can solve the problem in record time, intense exhaustion is setting in, as if I have been up for multiple days without sleep.

Once the EEG was in progress, the doctor confirmed his suspicions, and the correct prescriptions were in my hand before Marisa was coherent enough to leave the ER. I am exceedingly happy to report that since this time, with the proper medication added, Marisa has remained seizure-free since 2011.

By the time Tom landed, he was informed of the new diagnosis and the promise of new medication. He was relieved, and although both of us were exhausted from worrying, we were very happy and grateful for God's protection.

Chapter 18

Understanding Heaven

According to Google, the word *heaven* is mentioned 327 times in the New Testament (KJV) and 255 times in the Old Testament. After all, that is our goal, correct? It's our ultimate destination. As discussed earlier, our salvation is a free gift, one we all fall short of deserving. But it demands accepting Jesus as our Lord and Savior. It is only through this acceptance that his divine blood and God's ultimate plan to free us from sin can work for us. The free gift, which cannot be earned by works is summed up in one word   *grace*. It is through grace (acceptance of Jesus as God's son who suffered to become sin so our sins might die with him) that we are saved from being separated from God because of sin.

When Jesus wanted to educate his followers, he often spoke in parables. A parable was a made-up story to teach an important lesson or concept. One parable Jesus told his followers to further explain what the kingdom of heaven is like was the parable of the vineyard workers, found in Matthew 20:1–16 (NIV).

A landowner goes out early in the morning and hires men, agreeing to pay them a daily rate of a denarius, or silver coin, for a day's work in his vineyard. He hires them at various times during the day–9:00 a.m., twelve noon, 3:00 p.m., and 5:00 p.m., promising them all a fair wage.

When the end of the day comes, the landowner tells the manager to pay the workers, starting with those who came last. Following the landowner's directions, the manager gives the 5:00 p.m. workers a silver coin.

The workers who had been hired first thought that they would be getting paid extra because they had been working the longest. They, too, are given one silver coin as a daily wage. They immediately begin to grumble.

The landowner does not listen to their complaints and reminds them they agreed to the daily rate of pay. The landowner asks, "Am I not allowed to do what I choose with what belongs to me? Are you envious because I am generous?" The landowner then says, "The last shall be first, and the first shall be last."

What does this say about heaven?

This parable means that there are many Christians, like myself, who were born into Christianity and have been living for the kingdom since an early age. This means they have been attending church, volunteering, donating money to the church, giving to charitable causes, fasting, and so on. Fast-forward to others who accept Jesus as their Lord and Savior late in life and, in some circumstances, on their deathbeds. This parable demonstrates that mature Christians, as well as newborn Christians, are all guaranteed a place in heaven through *grace*.

Remember, according to New Testament Scripture, salvation cannot be earned. It is a gift. But in our humanness, we might complain that equal status is unjust, since one group put forth so much effort, and the last group just gave an oral confirmation that God so loved the world that he gave his one and only Son, that whoever believes in him shall not perish but have eternal life (John 3:16, NIV).

There are twenty-three parables all told by Jesus to educate his followers about God's expectations of them, as well as life's valuable, life-enhancing lessons. It is my hope that you will want to Google them, realizing that the Bible is not as intimidating as you once thought. Maybe you have vowed to take God's word off your bookshelf, dust it off, and crack it open. Perhaps my God-inspired words have convinced you that the New Testament is still relevant and very helpful to get through life—especially the difficult times.

An important note—there are dozens upon dozens of religions that do not acknowledge Jesus at all. Some, such as Islam and Judaism, believe him to be a great messenger or profit but certainly not the Son of God. I believe that there are good people in these groups who live for God and are focused on atoning for their sins through fasting, prayer, and sacrifice. Paradise at the end of a righteous life can and will be theirs; it just may or may not be through the gates of heaven. It could be a different section of paradise or in another location or dimension all together.

I had a glorious dream that I had passed on. I was inside of heaven, and I enjoyed total peace of heart, mind, and soul. All around me was much excitement; a trip was being offered to both the promised land of the Jews and to the paradise of Islam. Both places were highly rated and greatly anticipated. It added to our gratitude as Christians that God loves his children with so much intensity that he has found a way to save all who have done their best to lead a godly life by following his commandments and humbling themselves by recognizing the need for atonement.

I used to lie awake at night agonizing over my beloved Jewish friends who actively kept the sabbath holy and their food kosher, which, to me, is a very sacrificial, God-centered way of living life. I prayed to God for peace of mind and heart to know that they would not be coldly rejected at the heavenly gates because Jesus's blood is not redeemable to them.

Once again, I awoke from a dead sleep with my God-given answer, which was, "Don't worry about my chosen people. They are in constant atonement."

And then I remembered how faithful Muslims intermittently pray throughout the day and fast and follow the Qur'an and my anxiety faded away.

Ever since I received that message, my heart has been at peace. I learned to "let go and let God." He already has your tomorrows all figured out. Even so, let me implore you, if you consider yourself weak in your spiritual practices or are not inspired by your faith, do something to strengthen it. When your heart gets weak, does your cardiologist or general practitioner not recommend exercise to strengthen your heart? If exercise is too risky, they may recommend vitamins to nourish the heart. Is exercising once a week enough? Of course not! Is taking a vitamin once a week enough to improve a weak heart? Of course not! Going to church once a week is not enough to nourish a growing relationship with God either.

What would happen if you only spent one hour per week with your significant other? If you didn't call or write to each other between visits, your relationship would be destined to fail.

This truth became evident to me when I started attending a weekly Bible study. The 90-minute class was once a week, but I had at least three hours of homework, sometimes five. Then I programmed two Christian music radio stations into my audio list in my car. I also volunteered my time at my church that I continue to love and appreciate.

Then it happened. My heart was on fire, and my spirit was soaring! I was high on life the guiltless way, and I knew I would find that "narrow gate" that scripture warns few people find. I also became mindful that I was fulfilling God's hope for every Christian—to evolve from a young, immature Christian to a wise, mature Christian.

According to the apostle Paul, spiritual maturity is achieved through becoming more like Jesus Christ. According to Paul, it is an ongoing process that should never end in life. We start out as "baby Christians," and to that group he outlines Christianity in the simplest of ways, because that is what this group is most capable of understanding. As we grow in Christianity and become more educated in his words, our understanding increases, as does our wisdom. And we slowly become more like Christ! (1 Corinthians 2, LEB). Don't take that the wrong way—becoming more Christlike improves your quality of life; it doesn't diminish it.

According to James 4:8, "As we take steps closer to God, we experience His goodness, grace and glory in our lives in new ways."

In conclusion, as I finish this book, it is my hope that it will continue to guide future readers and offer hope to people who may have lost all optimism for human life due to a personal injury or serious illness. I hope my future family members will understand the person I was and evolved into during my short time on this earth.

I hope that I live long enough to get to know my future grandchildren, who I have loved for many years before they even came to be. I plan to love my grandchildren greatly and hope that they may love me as much as I loved my grandmother.

I hope to be waiting for you on the other side with open arms and a "tell-all" smile that rejoices in God's kept promises for us. We will have conquered death and will be free of life's heartaches and the physical pains our human body has endured. Our minds and spiritual bodies are perfect and designed to function flawlessly for an eternity. Yes, our Master Creator loves us that much. Do I get an "Amen"?

Made in United States
North Haven, CT
28 June 2023

38298800R00095